INTERCULTURAL COMMUNICATION WORKBOOK

THIRD EDITION

INTERCULTURAL COMMUNICATION WORKBOOK

THIRD EDITION

FRED E. JANDT
with DERRICK J. TABERSKI

Sage Publications, Inc.
International Educational and Professional Publisher
Thousand Oaks ■ London ■ Now Delhi

For information:

 Sage Publications, Inc.
2455 Teller Road
Thousand Oaks, California 91320
E-mail: order@sagepub.com

Sage Publications Ltd.
6 Bonhill Street
London EC2A 4PU
United Kingdom

Sage Publications India Pvt. Ltd.
M-32 Market
Greater Kailash I
New Delhi 110 048 India

Printed in the United States of America

ISBN 0-7619-2286-5

This book is printed on acid-free paper.

01 02 03 10 9 8 7 6 5 4 3 2 1

Acquiring Editor:	Margaret H. Seawell
Editorial Assistant:	Heidi Van Middlesworth
Production Editor:	Joyce Kuhn
Copy Editor:	Joyce Kuhn
Designer/Typesetter:	Janelle LeMaster
Cover Designer:	Ravi Balasuriya
Print Buyer:	Scott Hooper

Contents

CHAPTER 1

The Dispute Over Defining Culture

Many of us take our culture for granted. The only time that we may ever think about it is when we leave our own country to travel abroad or when we encounter someone with a culture so different from ours that we are forced to examine our own beliefs. Much of what we think is the "right" or "correct" way to act or to do something is actually part of the knowledge that we have learned from our culture. In other words, our culture teaches us rules or norms that tell us how to behave inside our culture. The word "culture" describes everything that makes a large group of people unique. Members of a culture share similar thoughts and experiences. One's culture is part of one's identity and is taught to one's children. Culture also includes all the things that guide a group of people through life, such as myths, language and gestures, ways of communicating, economic systems, what kinds of things to eat, and how to dress.

People identify with being a member of a group. Being a member of a group helps define who we are. We all are members of groups of different sizes. One of the largest groups that a person can belong to is a culture. Everyone belongs to a culture. No one chooses which culture to belong to. We simply are born into one.

Other groups that people may be a member of are subcultures (sometimes called co-cultures) and subgroups. Subcultures can be based on race, ethnicity, economic or social class, or geographic region. Some people think of race as a group of people descended from the same ancestors. Another definition of race is that it is sociohistorical in that it recognizes how categories of race have changed over time and how different cultures have different racial categories. Because of how the words used to identify people by race have changed, people can be born one race and die another. Ethnicity is a word that describes the shared descent or heritage of a group of people. Groups of people with the same ethnicity share the same cultural traits like language, religion, and customs that are passed on to the children. In very homogeneous cultures where there is little difference in race or ethnicity, people might identify with groups that have about the same degree of wealth or that live in the same area as they do.

Subgroups also help define who we are. Subgroups can be as small as a few people or as large as a major religion. For example, a high school student might identify with being a member of the football team or drama club, or a person might identify with being a Christian, a Buddhist, or a Jew. People can be members of many different groups at the same time, so a person might identify with being a Christian, a football player, and a member of the drama club. Subgroups also provide their members with norms that tell people how to behave and even think. So, for instance, a Christian cannot be a Buddhist because Christians have rules that tell them they cannot be members of a different religion. People often make friendships based on their memberships in subgroups.

Business and politics constantly bring people of different cultural groups into contact with each other. Immigration is also a factor that continues to bring different cultures together. Knowledge of the norms of different cultures can help people to better communicate across cultures. It is possible through immigration and marriage to have members of the same family be members of different cultures. One day, your intercultural communication skills might even help you to talk with your in-laws.

Purposes

1. To discover how your culture affects how you define your family
2. To understand how family background affects how you communicate

Instructions

1. A family tree is a genealogical chart showing the ancestry and relationship of all members of a family. Make a family tree that shows three or more generations of your family. Use any information that is available to you, such as family records and conversations with older members of your family. Include when and where your family members were born (dates and places of birth). Also include the dates that anyone migrated from one country to another.

2. Use the information from your family tree to answer the questions in the "Conclusions" section.

Conclusions

1. How did you decide who to include in your family tree? Think about how you defined the concept "family." Consider the use of the family name (e.g., father's last name, both mother's and father's last name).

2. How do you think other cultures define family? Think of ways to define family that are different from the way that you defined it.

3. How did influences outside of your family affect your family tree (e.g., cultural expectations about size of families, government policies, war, religion)?

4. What were the reasons for any migration? What influenced the decision to stay in a country?

5. In what ways has your family background affected how you communicate?

EXERCISE 1.2: FOOD NORMS

Purpose

To recognize that food habits are an important part of cultural identity. Every culture has its own culinary traditions: Danish roast goose and red cabbage, Mexico's tamales, and Polish baked or fried fish and herring in sour cream. Many U.S. holiday feasts were actually staples in the indigenous diet—sweet potatoes, squash, corn, and cranberries.

Instructions

1. Keep a journal of all the food that you eat in one day.
2. Write down the recipe for a special dish that is unique to your family background (e.g., something that your family eats only on special occasions like holidays or other special times).
3. Answer the questions at the end of this exercise.

Food Journal for the Day: _____

Time	Circumstances (what, where, with whom, etc.)

Conclusions

1. How does the food in your journal reflect your culture? Think about what you ate, when you ate, with whom you ate, and how you ate the food.

2. Food habits remain in a family even after other elements of culture are gone. What aspects of culture are reflected in your family food recipe?

3. List some common foods in your country that have been borrowed from other cultures. Example: croissant from France.

Purpose

To practice using exchange rates

Instructions

Use the currency exchange rates listed in the business section of the newspaper or the Internet to figure out the U.S. dollar costs of the following items.

A dress that costs 3,000 baht in Thailand is $ _____.

A table setting that costs 1,210 krone in Denmark is $ _____.

A cap that costs 5 pounds in Ireland is $ _____.

Shoes that cost 51,120 lire in Italy are $ _____.

A swimsuit that costs 499 francs in France is $ _____.

A fax machine that costs 2,340 Hong Kong dollars is $ _____.

▣ **EXERCISE 1.4: FRIENDSHIP CHOICE**

Purpose

To recognize the effect of cultural, social class, ethnic, and subgroup identity on friendship choice

Instructions

1. List your 10 best friends by name below. For this exercise, a friend is someone to whom you tell the most personal information about yourself. Also, you know a lot of personal information about them.

2. Next, identify these friends by their group memberships. These should be the groups that you consider the most important in your relationship with that person. They may be culture, social class, ethnic, or subgroup.

Friend's Name	Friend's Group Memberships
Example: Fred	Star Trek fan club, fraternity, Spanish major, international student club
1.	
2.	
3.	
4.	
5.	
6.	
7.	
8.	
9.	
10.	

Conclusions

1. How many of your friends are of the same or similar group? Are you a member of this group, too?

2. If you have any friends who do not share similar group memberships with you, what is the basis of the friendship?

3. In what ways, if any, is communication different between friends of your group and those not of your group? Recall the story in Box 1.2: Personalizing the Concept. How do people who have shared the same experiences communicate? How is this different from those who have not shared the same or similar experiences?

SOURCE: Based on Richard W. Brislin, "Increasing Awareness of Class, Ethnicity, Culture, and Race by Expanding on Students' Own Experiences," in I. Cohen (Ed.), *The G. Stanley Hall Lecture Series*, Vol. 8 (Washington, DC: American Pyschological Association, 1988).

◙ **EXERCIJE 1.5: GROUP MEMBERJHIPJ**

Purposes

1. To help you recognize the many cultural groups and subgroups to which you belong
2. To help you identify the norms (rules of behavior) that are provided us by various groups

Instructions

1. Make a list of all the groups you identify with. Consider nationality, ethnicity, geographic region, interests, and hobbies (for example, U.S., German-American, Californian, surfing, and skiing).

2. Give an example of a norm for each group. Remember that a norm is an action and not a value.

Group	Sample Norm
Example: Japanese	Don't ask questions in class

Conclusion

We all participate in many groups. Sometimes, we even participate in many groups at the same time (e.g., members of a fraternity playing basketball). Which groups do you identify with most? Which groups' norms do you follow the most?

EXERCISE 1.6: NORMS AROUND THE WORLD   ▣

Purpose

To recognize diverse cultural norms

Instructions

1. To test your knowledge of cultural customs, answer the following questions. Check your answers against those in the Answer section at the end of the workbook.
2. Answer the questions that follow the test.

1. People eat with a fork in their left hand in which country?
    a. South Africa
    b. United Kingdom
    c. Indonesia
    d. The Netherlands
    e. All of the above
2. In which country do members of the dominant religion not eat pork (meat that comes from pigs)?
    a. Saudi Arabia
    b. Egypt
    c. Malaysia
    d. Indonesia
    e. All of the above
3. People usually eat dinner
    a. at about 5 pm in South Africa
    b. at about 7 pm in Indonesia, Switzerland, and Malaysia
    c. at about 8 pm in Italy and France
    d. after 9 pm in Spain
    e. All of the above
4. Before entering a South Korean's home, you should remove your shoes and wait to be invited in.
    a. True
    b. False
5. In England, to "table an issue or motion" means to
    a. not talk about it until later
    b. bring it up and discuss it now
    c. ignore it
6. In which country is it polite to use both hands to pass an object to somebody?
    a. Germany
    b. Canada
    c. South Korea
    d. Russia
    e. All of the above
7. When discussing business with a person from a Latin American or Asian country, if you try to maintain eye contact with that person, he or she will think that you are
    a. honest and truthful
    b. aggressive
    c. attentive

8. In which country should you carry a large quantity of business cards (in English and the language of the country) and give one to everyone you meet?
   a. Korea
   b. Japan
   c. China
   d. Taiwan
   e. All of the above

9. In which country would you not expect to be told directly that your work was bad?
   a. Japan
   b. China
   c. Taiwan
   d. Malaysia
   e. All of the above

10. In Saudi Arabia, it is not polite to admire an object while your host is with you because he may feel that he must give it to you.
   a. True
   b. False

11. When talking, South Americans, Africans, and Arabs usually stand closer together than people from other cultures do. If you back away from them, they may think that you do not like them or that you are not interested in what they want to say.
   a. True
   b. False

12. During the month of Ramadan, Muslims do not eat during the daytime. While in their presence you should not
   a. eat
   b. smoke
   c. drink alcohol
   d. All of the above

13. Friday is the official day of rest in which country?
   a. Pakistan
   b. Jordan
   c. Somalia
   d. Kuwait
   e. All of the above

14. In Islamic countries, women must wear clothing that will cover up their arms and legs and hide their body shape.
   a. True
   b. False

15. When in Saudi Arabia, you should not
   a. discuss women
   b. discuss politics
   c. discuss religion
   d. refer to the Persian Gulf as the Arab Gulf
   e. All of the above

16. Saturday is the official day of rest in which country?
   a. Egypt
   b. Israel
   c. Tunisia
   d. Syria
   e. None of the above

17. Seven is a lucky number in the United States but an unlucky number in Ghana, Kenya, and Singapore.
    a. True
    b. False

18. Potato chips manufactured by the Wise Corporation, with its owl trademark, probably will not be sold in
    a. India because the owl is a sign of bad luck
    b. England because of the color of its packaging
    c. Canada because of the shape of the chip
    d. France because of its packaging and shape

19. In which region of the world is it acceptable to hire a member of your family?
    a. East Asia
    b. Latin America
    c. Arabian countries
    d. All of the above
    e. None of the above

20. In which country do people think that it is unsanitary to have a toilet and bathing facilities in the same room?
    a. Ireland
    b. Japan
    c. Venezuela
    d. Oman
    e. None of the above

21. In which country does a man greet a woman by placing the palms of both hands together and bowing slightly?
    a. China
    b. Taiwan
    c. South Korea
    d. Malaysia
    e. India

22. In which country would a person greet an elder by bowing lower and longer than the older person?
    a. China
    b. Taiwan
    c. Brazil
    d. Japan
    e. Indonesia

23. In which country do people greet each other with a slight bow followed by a handshake?
    a. China
    b. Taiwan
    c. Brazil
    d. Indonesia
    e. All of the above

24. When shaking hands, which of the following is true?
    a. In France, it includes a light grasp and a quick, crisp handshake.
    b. In China, a pumping handshake conveys pleasure.
    c. Among Arabs, the handshake is limp and long.
    d. Among South African Blacks, the handshake is followed by clenched thumbs and then another handshake.
    e. All of the above

25. Men do not shake hands with women in
    a. South Korea
    b. India
    c. Saudi Arabia
    d. Thailand
    e. All of the above

Your number correct: _____

Conclusions

1. How did your score compare to others? Why were some people more familiar with the norms of other cultures?

2. How could you improve your knowledge of the norms of other countries?

3. What problems in communication could arise from not knowing the norms of other countries?

SOURCE: The test questions were developed by William A. Nowlin, Associate Professor of Management in the College of Business at the Rochester (New York) Institute of Technology, and printed in *Southwest Airlines Spirit*, May 1990, pp. 33, 36, and 95, and June 1990, pp. 27, 30, and 89. Published by East/West Network, Inc., 34 East 51st Street, New York, NY 10022. Reprinted courtesy of Southwest SPIRIT, carried aboard Southwest Airlines © 1990; East/West Network, Publisher and AA Magazine Publications.

CHAPTER 2

Defining Communication as an Element of Culture

When communicating with people from different cultures, it is important to remember that culture and communication are strongly connected. The way that people view communication—what it is, how to do it, and reasons for doing it—is part of their culture. The chance of misunderstanding between members of different cultures increases when this important connection is forgotten.

In general, people from Western and Asian cultures have the greatest chance of misunderstanding each other. Much of this misunderstanding comes from the fact that the Western and Asian cultures have two very different views of communication. Western cultures, especially the United States, give higher status to the speaker or "source" of information than to the "receiver" or person who pays attention to the information. The source encodes a message (information that the source wants to share with other people) by putting it into symbols (usually words or nonverbal gestures), and then sends it through a channel. A channel can be print media like magazines and newspapers, electronic media like television, radio, and the Internet, or sounds traveling through the air when two people speak face-to-face. Sometimes, things make it difficult for the message to reach the receiver. These things are called "noise." Noise can be physical (e.g., loud sound), emotional (e.g., strong feelings like sadness or anxiety), or biological (e.g. like when you are hungry or sick). When receivers get the message, they must "decode" or try to understand it. For example, if the source encodes a message using English, the receivers must use their knowledge of the English language to understand it. Often, the source pays attention to the reactions of the receivers. This information or feedback from the receiver is called "receiver response."

Asian cultures view communication as communicators cooperating to make meaning. This model of communication reflects Confucian collectivist values because respecting the relationship through communication can be more important than the information that is exchanged.

In intercultural communication situations, it is natural for people to be aware of the potential for various misunderstandings and to want to avoid them. However, despite the best intentions, serious misunderstanding and even conflicts can occur. One reason for this is that even though people are consciously attempting to avoid problems, they still are making ethical judgments as they are communicating. The values that people hold affect both their communication decisions and interpretation of what others communicate.

Western and Asian cultures often have the greatest misunderstandings when ethics are considered. For example, an Asian who had a Confucian view of communication would think it perfectly acceptable to give gifts to business associates and to hire one's own relatives. Both of these actions help maintain social relationships. However, people in the United States would consider these actions bribery and nepotism, both of which are against the law in the United States. So, differing ethics can cause conflicts, especially when what one culture may consider morally wrong, another may actually encourage. When such conflicts occur, people who want to be ethical intercultural communicators should try to understand, respect, and accept each individual's ethical perspective.

Good intercultural communicators have personality strength (strong sense of self and are socially relaxed), communication skills (verbal and nonverbal), psychological adjustment (ability to adapt to new situations), and cultural awareness (understanding how people of different cultures think and act).

These areas can be divided into eight different skills: self-awareness (using knowledge about yourself to deal with difficult situations), self-respect (confidence in what you think, feel, and do), interaction (how effectively you communicate with people), empathy (being able to see and feel things from other people's points of view), adaptability (how fast you can adjust to new situations and norms), certainty (the ability to do things opposite to what you feel), initiative (being open to new situations), and acceptance (being tolerant or accepting of unfamiliar things).

EXERCISE 2.1: INTERCULTURAL COMMUNICATION
ETHICS: RAJPAL AND BALBIR

Purpose

To consider how ethics apply in intercultural settings

Instructions

Read the following case study and answer the questions that follow.

In South Asian cultures, the most important social unit is the extended family. Unlike the nuclear family, which includes only a married couple and their children, the extended family includes relatives—aunts, uncles, cousins, and grandparents. When families immigrate to a new country, they still keep the values and behavior associated with the extended family. For example, decisions for the entire extended family usually are made by one person, generally the most financially secure male. Also, the individual incomes of the family members are often added together and spent on behalf of the entire family.

Within the family, gender roles are well defined in South Asian cultures. Men are the leaders. They make the major decisions, provide for the family, and are the heads of the family. Women are generally submissive and obedient. Their job is to take care of the family and perform household duties. Still, women do have high status because they bear the family honor.

Marriages are still frequently arranged, and divorce is very rare in traditional South Asian cultures. There is strong pressure on couples to stay together as divorce will reflect badly upon the whole family. The brothers and sisters of a woman who left her husband will find it difficult to arrange marriages for themselves. Because divorce is not an acceptable course of action, these cultures have established other ways to deal with marital problems. In India, for example, the traditional method of mediation involves male elders considering the conflict, deciding who is guilty, and then deciding how the wife and/or husband should change their behavior to correct the problem. The mediators may independently gather facts, but they may not talk with the woman.

Case Study

Rajpal, a woman of South Asian descent, was born in India but raised in the United States. Growing up in the United States, she acquired many U.S. values and customs. When she was 18, she married Balbir, a man who was raised in India and whom she had never met prior to the marriage. Now they have been married for three and one-half years. However, Rajpal is unhappy with her marriage. She has told her family how she feels, but they have blamed her for the failing marriage. Balbir has traditional Indian expectations of the relationship. The marriage is acceptable to him. He wants to have a stable family so that he can sponsor his parents as immigrants.

Rajpal asks you to intervene as a mediator. She tells you that they have totally different backgrounds and that Balbir dictates what she should do.

Questions

1. What is your response to Rajpal's request? How does the fact that they are living in the United States affect your interpretation of the situation?

2. What ethical considerations guide your decision?

SOURCE: Case study developed by Fred E. Jandt from "Culture and Conflict in Canada: Tradition and Transition," by Michelle LeBaron, in Fred E. Jandt and Paul B. Pedersen (Eds.), *Constructive Conflict Management: Asia-Pacific Cases* (Thousand Oaks, CA: Sage Publications, 1996), pp. 63-75. May not be duplicated.

EXERCISE 2.2: INTERCULTURAL COMMUNICATION COMPETENCE ◙

Purpose

To help you assess your intercultural communication competence at the beginning of the course

Instructions

1. Answer each question as you honestly believe you would react. Choose only one answer for each question.
2. There is a scoring guide following the questionnaire. Note the number of points for each selection, then add the points from each pair of questions, and transfer that total to the chart following the guide.
3. Use the questions in the "Conclusions" section to help you interpret your score.

1. You want to take a picture of a child. You take out your camera, but just as you are about to take the picture, an old man quickly comes over and starts shouting at you.
   a. You hesitate and decide not to photograph that child, but you look around for another child to photograph.
   b. You are aware that the old man does not want you to take the photo. You can't understand why, but you apologize and put your camera away.
   c. You wait until you think the man can't see you and then take the picture anyway.
2. You are visiting a holy temple and notice shoes lined up outside the door.
   a. You walk into the temple with your shoes on because it seems silly to you to take them off.
   b. You take off your shoes like you have seen other people do and then walk into the temple.
   c. You hesitate as you are about to enter and then decide not to go in because you don't want to take your shoes off.
3. Assume you are a heterosexual man living in another country. You tell your friend, who is a native citizen of that country, that you were promoted in your job. He congratulates you by giving you a warm hug.
   a. You accept the hug and hug him back, thanking him for his congratulations. You offer to buy him a cup of coffee.
   b. You're startled, but you let him hug you. However, you are a bit embarrassed about it and your actions show it.
   c. You are embarrassed, so you push him away and assume that he is a homosexual.
4. You have been living and working in Greenoch, Scotland, for over a year, but now your company wants you to move to their offices in New London. Some people from Glasgow (a few friends and some friends of friends) invite you to a restaurant there. You arrive and find a farewell party in your honor. There are flowers, music, and wine. One of the guests whom you have never met before hands you a gift.
   a. You thank him for the gift and feel pretty good about yourself and what you did while you were in Scotland.
   b. You thank him but tell him that you can't accept the gift because your company does not allow you to accept gifts from the local people.
   c. You thank him but while you are talking later with one of your Scottish friends, you make fun of the stranger because you think it was stupid for him to give a gift to someone he had never met before.

MORE

5. You ask directions with much difficulty in a foreign language; the person you ask directs you to the wrong place.
   a. You decide that from now on you will always ask two or three people for directions.
   b. You get very angry and assume that the man gave you the wrong directions on purpose. You decide to avoid asking the native people for advice in the future.
   c. When you end up at the wrong place, you assume you asked the question incorrectly or you misunderstood when the man answered you. You decide to ask directions from someone who can speak your native language from now on.

6. Assume you are a man who has been out on a date with a village girl. It had been an enjoyable evening, and you think that she likes you. However, when you try to kiss her good night, she pushes you away and runs into her house, slamming the door behind her. You
   a. assume that she is "cold" and that she doesn't like people from your country.
   b. realize that it must not be the custom in this culture to kiss on the first date. You plan to phone her tomorrow, apologize, and ask for another date.
   c. assume that you have done something wrong during the evening; maybe she didn't enjoy the date as much as you did.

7. You are about to enter a restaurant in a foreign city. Near the door is an old woman who looks as if she hasn't eaten for many days. She comes up to you with her hand extended, begging for money.
   a. You put a coin into her hand, look at her, and wish her a good day.
   b. You push her aside and tell her to leave you alone.
   c. You toss a coin at her and go quickly into the restaurant without looking back.

8. You are in a Spanish town with an African-American friend. You enter a local bar that mostly serves tourists. You notice that there are only two kinds of music: Spanish and country-western. You friend tells you that he wished the bar had rap music.
   a. You insist that the bar owner play some rap music for your friend.
   b. You tell your friend he can either listen to Spanish music or leave without you.
   c. You have a conversation about music with the bar owner and point out to him that he might get more business if he included some rap records. You say you'd like to stay longer, but your friend is getting bored, and you leave together.

9. You are in Athens and need to change some of your money to drachmae (Greek currency). You enter a store and show a bill to the cashier, and she jerks her head up and down as if (in your opinion) to say "OK." You hand her the money. She looks puzzled and hands it back.
   a. You figure that she doesn't like people of your nationality, give her a dirty look, and leave.
   b. You give her the money back again and add a little extra for a tip.
   c. You find a Greek who speaks your language to help you.

10. You've invited a local businessman and his family to your home for dinner. The food is prepared and ready by 7:30 pm, but your guests don't arrive until 9:30. You try to keep the food warm until they come, but you end up burning it.
    a. You don't say anything. You serve your guests their plate of burned food, but in your mind you blame them for what happened to the food.
    b. You are angry and tell your guests how rude they have been to you.
    c. You offer refreshments, suggesting that you all go out to your favorite restaurant. You tell them that you ruined the meal, and you're very sorry.

11. In a foreign city you are a passenger on a bus crowded with many people. You have to get off at the next stop. You signal the bus driver, and he slows the bus down but doesn't stop. You jump off while the bus is still moving past your stop.
    a. You are puzzled and decide that next time you will watch other people getting off buses to see how they signal the driver to stop.
    b. You shrug your shoulders and walk away.
    c. You become angry at the bus driver and yell a few bad words at the bus as it departs.

12. The oldest son of a local family invites you to his home to meet the rest of his family. Another guest, an elderly man who is also a local resident, arrives at the same time you do. You both enter the room where the family is waiting. The other guest greets the grandfather, then the father, and finally the son. It is now your turn to introduce yourself.
    a. You greet your host and hope he will introduce you to the rest of the family and the guest.
    b. You hesitate, then turn and greet the family in the same order as you saw the guest do.
    c. You notice that the other guest greeted the grandfather and father first, but you assume they have met before. You greet your host first.

13. At a party at the home of a host national (native resident of a country) you are watching people do some local dances. Suddenly your host takes you by the hand and asks you to join the dancing.
    a. You get up reluctantly, stiffly try a few steps to please him but quickly sit down again.
    b. You shake you head "no" because you don't want to make a fool of yourself.
    c. You get up, glad you've been asked to join the festivities. Even though you're not very good, you try the steps and stay up for the next dance.

14. In a foreign town you board a bus, take your seat, and the person next to you smiles a greeting.
    a. You smile, nod your head, and say hello. You try to begin a conversation in the language of the country, even though you realize that your vocabulary is limited to only a few words.
    b. You smile back and nod hello, hoping the passenger won't want to talk to you.
    c. You look away and pretend that you didn't see him because you don't want to try to talk to him.

15. You are at a bar. You need to use the rest room. You ask a bartender to tell you where it is. He points to the exit. You walk outside and find no rest room, only the wall of the building. Many men and some women are using the wall as a toilet.
    a. You are disgusted and decide to go back to your hotel.
    b. You decide to wait because you would be embarrassed to expose yourself. You go back to the bar.
    c. You decide that this is the custom, and you join the others at the wall.

16. You are walking to a nearby village when you see a couple going in the same direction as you. The peasant woman has some heavy-looking baskets tied to her back, and the man walking with her is carrying nothing.
    a. You walk up to the couple and offer to carry some of the load. The man vigorously shakes his head and motions for you to leave.
    b. You go up to the man and yell at him for treating his woman like a packhorse.
    c. Although you feel sorry for the woman, you assume this is the custom. You greet the couple and walk on, figuring it's not your place to interfere.

Scoring Guide

1. a = 2, b = 3, c = 1   5. a = 3, b = 1, c = 2   9. a = 0, b = 1, c = 3   13. a = 2, b = 1, c = 3
2. a = 1, b = 3, c = 2   6. a = 1, b = 3, c = 2   10. a = 2, b = 1, c = 3   14. a = 3, b = 1, c = 0
3. a = 3, b = 2, c = 1   7. a = 3, b = 0, c = 1   11. a = 3, b = 2, c = 1   15. a = 1, b = 2, c = 3
4. a = 3, b = 0, c = 1   8. a = 2, b = 0, c = 3   12. a = 2, b = 3, c = 1   16. a = 2, b = 1, c = 3

Add up your score for each pair of questions and circle the total:

Self-awareness (Questions 1 and 2):	0 1 2 3 4 5 6
Self-respect (Questions 3 and 4):	0 1 2 3 4 5 6
Interaction (Questions 5 and 6):	0 1 2 3 4 5 6
Empathy (Questions 7 and 8):	0 1 2 3 4 5 6
Adaptability (Questions 9 and 10):	0 1 2 3 4 5 6
Certainty (Questions 11 and 12):	0 1 2 3 4 5 6
Initiative (Questions 13 and 14):	0 1 2 3 4 5 6
Acceptance (Questions 15 and 16):	0 1 2 3 4 5 6

MORE

Conclusions

1. Go back and reread Questions 7 and 8. These questions are used as an assessment of empathy. Empathy here is defined as responding from an understanding of another person's perspective and feelings. Notice, though, that if you acted differently out of respect for the local culture's customs, your score would be low. Comment on this contradiction. What other intercultural communication skill areas affect the empathy score?

2. The higher the number, the greater your skill in this area. Which areas do you need to improve?

3. Consider your weak skill areas. Briefly describe a few situations that you have been in where your lack of skill caused communication problems. What could you have done to improve the situations?

SOURCE: Adapted from *Overseas Diplomacy: Guidelines for United States Navy* and excerpted in David S. Hoopes and Paul Ventura (Eds.), *Intercultural Sourcebook: Cross-Cultural Training Methodologies* (Chicago: Intercultural Press, 1979), pp. 89-101.

CHAPTER 3

Barriers to Intercultural Communication

If you have ever watched street performers, chances are you've seen a mime doing a routine known as "trapped in an imaginary box." At the beginning of the routine, the mime goes in one direction. Suddenly, the mime hits an imaginary wall. Curious, the mime touches the wall and searches for a way around it but cannot find one. The mime then goes in different directions, but after a few steps hits another invisible wall each time. The mime is trapped. The only ways out are to either end the show or to imagine some clever escape. Similarly, in intercultural communication settings, it is all too easy to become trapped by invisible walls or barriers to communication. Although these walls are hard to perceive, they are not imaginary. The only way to "escape" is to learn to see them and avoid making the communication mistakes that come from them.

There are six barriers to communication—anxiety, assuming similarities instead of differences, ethnocentrism, stereotypes and prejudice, nonverbals, and language problems. Anxiety is feeling nervous, which can affect communication when you focus so much on your own feelings that you do not pay attention to what other people are telling you. If you are speaking to someone in your second language, you may worry that the other person may speak too fast or will use words you do not understand. Anxiety may also affect your ability to communicate your ideas to others. If you are in a situation where you feel very nervous, such as talking to your boss, you may find yourself saying awkward things or even making mistakes in grammar that you never do when talking with your friends.

Assuming similarities instead of differences is a natural thing to do if you do not have any information about a culture. Assuming that a culture is similar to your own can cause you to ignore important differences. It does not help to do the opposite—that is, to assume that everything is different—because this will lead to overlooking important similarities between cultures. The best thing to do when you encounter a new culture is to assume nothing and to ask what the customs are.

Ethnocentrism is negatively judging another culture by your own culture's standards. To make ethnocentric judgments is to believe that the ways of your own culture are better than those of others. Although ethnocentrism is considered a barrier to communication, it is common for people experiencing "culture shock" to make these kinds of judgments. When learning a new culture, individuals may go through a stage when they consider everything about the new culture to be worse than their home culture. However, after this stage, individuals usually begin to see one culture as not better or worse than another but as merely different.

Even though modern communication technology allows people access to increasing amounts of information about things happening all over the world, there is still a tendency for people to be more interested in local, state, and national news. In the United States, the most popular news shows do not cover international events in as much detail or accuracy as they do national and local news. It is common for people to form opinions about other countries using only the knowledge acquired through the media.

Even though there may be many ties between countries, such as those between the United States and Japan, international travelers still often find that things are very different from what they had expected, which sometimes leads to feelings of anxiety.

◨ **EXERCISE 3.1: RECOGNIZING INTERCULTURAL BARRIERS**

Purpose

To recognize barriers that can occur in intercultural communication situations

Instructions

Read each of the situations presented below. Then determine what barrier or barriers were present in the situation. The possible barriers are anxiety, assuming similarities instead of differences, and ethnocentrism. What should the communication source or receiver have done to have avoided this situation? What should they each do now?

1. A kindergarten boy from India was teased and called "garbage head" by his classmates who noticed the smell of coconut oil on his hair.

Barrier: _____

2. An increasing number of immigrants to an area served by a large urban school led its principal to start a program in which older student volunteers would tutor younger children from immigrant families in the families' homes. The principal hoped that the program would help the new students adjust more rapidly to school life and increase their parents' confidence in the school. A 17-year-old student, John, was assigned to tutor a Chinese girl, Mee Loon, in English. Her father became concerned that the tutor was male and dressed strangely.

Barrier: _____

3. A United States college-age woman cleaned her dorm room while her Thai roommate was having breakfast in the dormitory dining hall. She did not know that in the Thai culture the head is sacred and putting a piece of clothing associated with a lesser part of the body on a place reserved for the head is one of the worst possible insults. The woman placed the Thai woman's skirt on the pillow portion of the bed. When the roommate returned, she became upset, cried, and left the room.

Barrier: _____

4. A frail, old, almost totally blind lady appeared at every health clinic session and sat on the dirt floor enjoying the activity. She was dirty and dishevelled and obviously had very little, even by Malaysian *kampong* (local village) standards. A nurse tried to obtain help for the woman. She was able to convince the Department of Welfare to give the old woman a small pension, which would provide the woman enough money to live on. However the woman continued to wear the same dirty dress and still looked like she did not have enough to eat. In squatting near her, the nurse noted a wad of bills in the woman's basket. "You have spent nothing. Why is that?" The woman laughed and explained, "I am saving it all for my funeral."

Barrier: _____

5. Two brothers and a sister, ages 7, 8, and 10, were expelled from their elementary school for nine months because they wore ceremonial daggers required by their religion. The children's parents explained that the dagger, called a *kirpan*, is one of five sacred symbols that must be worn at all times by baptized Khalsa Sikhs.

Barrier: _____

SOURCES: Situations adapted from *A Manual of Teaching Techniques for Intercultural Education* (Amherst: University of Massachusetts Press, 1971); Patricia G. Ramsey, *Teaching and Learning in a Diverse World: Multicultural Education for Young Children* (New York: Teachers College Press, 1987, p. 57); and Mildred Sikkema and Agnes Niyekawa, *Design for Cross-Cultural Learning* (Yarmouth, ME: Intercultural Press, Inc., 1987, p. 3).

▣ **EXERCIJE 3.2: INTERVIEWING INTERNATIONAL JTUDENTJ ON COMMUNICATION**

Purpose

To learn the communication problems an international student faces in the United States

Instructions

Interview an international student on the communication problems the student experienced in the United States. The following questions are suggested:

1. What specific communication problems did you encounter when you first came to the United States, and how did you handle them?

2. Describe your competency as a speaker of _____. Describe your competency as a speaker of English.

3. What do you wish you had learned or known before you came to the United States?

4. What things have we in the United States done or could still do to decrease the impact or severity of communication problems you have experienced?

5. What, if any, communication adjustments do you expect that you will have to make when you return to _____ ?

Conclusions

From this interview, what can you conclude about culture shock, acculturation, and intercultural communication competence?

Did you find it challenging to conduct this interview? If so, how were you challenged?

SOURCE: Adapted from Madeline M. Keaveney and Deborah Yurkovic, *Japanese Communication Practices and Strategies: A Pilot Study*, paper presented at Conference on Communication in Japan and the United States, March 14-15, 1991, California State University at Fullerton.

▣ **EXERCISE 3.3: ETHNOCENTRISM:
UNITED STATES AND CHINA**

Purposes

1. To recognize popular ethnocentristic judgments made about the Chinese by the people and government of the United States
2. To recognize ethnocentristic judgments made about the people and government in the United States by the Chinese
3. To recognize how those ethnocentristic judgments impede intercultural communication

> NOTE: If your native country is not the United States, consider the ethnocentric judgments that occur between your country and China.

Instructions

1. Whether or not you are a member of the group, identify commonly held ethnocentristic judgments made about the Chinese and ethnocentristic judgments made about the United States.
2. Give examples of media or other sources through which these judgments are spread.
3. Explain how those ethnocentristic judgments impede intercultural communication.

Ethnocentristic Judgments About the Chinese	Source	Effect
Example: Human rights are commonly violated	U.S. media reports of Tiananmien Square	Trade limits; China sees U.S. concern as an excuse to interfere in its affairs

Ethnocentristic Judgments About the United States	Source	Effect
Example: Racism and sexism	Marxist class-analysis	Give importance to political role of U.S. students

Conclusions

1. What have been the major ways these judgments have been spread?

2. How have the judgments impeded intercultural communication?

CHAPTER 4

Stereotypes and Prejudice as Barriers

Did you hear the one about the _____?" We will not go on. Jokes such as these help maintain a very strong barrier to communication—stereotypes and prejudice. Stereotyping is assuming that a person has certain qualities (good or bad) just because the person is a member of a specific group. An example of a stereotype is the belief that one group of people is stupid or that another produces good athletes. Prejudice is feeling hatred for or expressing suspicion toward people who belong to a certain group, race, religion, or sexual orientation. A specific kind of prejudice, racism, refers to having feelings of hatred for or expressing suspicion toward all members of a particular race and denying this group its rights.

Stereotyping and prejudice both have negative effects on communication. If a stereotype is very common, people may assume that it is true. Even the people who are stereotyped may eventually believe it, too. Stereotypes can have a negative effect when people use them to interpret behavior. Prejudice can have very serious effects, for it can lead to discrimination and hate crimes. Hate crime refers to hostile words and actions that people say or do against a certain group because that group is different.

Stereotypes, prejudice, and racism are learned from other people or institutions that are prejudiced. Prejudice continues to exist because of socialization and the apparent social, economic, and psychological benefits that come from it. Historically in the United States, there was a lot of prejudice against people who recently immigrated. After the huge wave of immigration that followed the Potato Famine in Ireland, there was much prejudice against Irish people in the United States because earlier immigrants worried that the new immigrants would take their jobs.

Although overtly prejudiced individuals and groups exist, governments, too, have encouraged prejudice in the citizens of their countries through the kinds of policies they have followed. In the United States during World War II, the government's propaganda against Germany and Japan caused much prejudice against people of German and Japanese ancestry. The internment of thousands of Japanese-Americans during the war also served to increase feelings of prejudice against this group. The United States is not the only government to allow such prejudice to exist. The Japanese policy of not allowing non-Japanese people to become citizens has created a second-class citizenry among Koreans living in Japan.

Stereotypes, prejudice, and racism continue to have a strong presence in the media. They can be found in print media, ranging from children's books to college brochures, and in electronic media. The movies and television programs of popular culture still portray many minorities and foreign groups in a stereotyped way.

EXERCISE 4.1: STEREOTYPES ABOUT THE UNITED STATES   ▣

Purposes

1. To recognize stereotypes that others may hold about the United States
2. To recognize how these stereotypes affect intercultural communication

Instructions

From your own experience and by interviewing others, make a list of commonly believed stereotypes about the United States. Example: People in the United States are rich.

Conclusions

1. How true are these stereotypes?

2. How do these stereotypes affect how people from other cultures communicate with people in the United States?

◙ **EXERCISE 4.2: LEARNINGS FROM CHILDHOOD**

Purposes

1. To become aware of the stereotypes you may have been exposed to as a child
2. To consider how these may have affected your communication behavior

Instructions

Our most intensive language and cultural learning takes place in childhood. At that time, we are taught how to relate to strangers. Think back on your own childhood to discover the things you were taught about people of different ethnic groups, different religions, and so on. Write down some stereotypes that you were taught, when and where you learned them, who taught them to you, and how they may have affected your communication behavior with individuals in that group.

Learning	When and Where I Learned It	Who Taught It to Me	Effect on My Behavior
Example: Poor people are lazy.	When I was 6 or 7	My parents	No sympathy for people on welfare

Conclusions

1. Did you recall only negative stereotypes? What positive stereotypes can you recall?

2. Do you still have the same beliefs? If not, then what caused them to change?

◙ **EXERCISE 4.3: STEREOTYPES IN BOOKS**

Purpose

To become more alert to stereotypes in books

Instructions

1. Select a textbook. You may want to find one for young children and one printed many years ago.

2. Using the guidelines below, evaluate the text for stereotypes of women, men, aged persons, ethnic groups, and so on.

NAME OF TEXTBOOK: _____   YEAR PUBLISHED: _____

BRIEF DESCRIPTION OF TEXTBOOK: _____

_____

_____

_____

1. Check the illustrations. Look for stereotypes. Who's doing what?

2. Check the story line. How are success and problems defined? What is the role of women?

3. Look at lifestyles. How are different groups shown?

4. Consider the relationships between people. Who has power? Who is subservient? Are certain family relationships assumed with particular groups?

5. Note the heroes and heroines. Who helps whom? Are any conflicts avoided?

6. Consider the effects on the reader's self-image. Does the reader come into contact with any norms that might limit the reader's aspirations and self-esteem?

7. Consider the author's and illustrator's qualifications.

8. Check out the author's perspective. What cultural, social, and economic perspectives does the book embody?

9. Watch for loaded words (words that try to bias the reader). Are there words with derogatory overtones and connotations?

10. Look at the copyright date. More recent books may more accurately present other points of view.

SOURCE: Adapted from "Ten Quick Ways to Analyze Children's Books for Racism and Sexism," in *Council on Interracial Books for Children Bulletin*, 1974, 5(3), 1-6.

EXERCISE 4.4: ΛRΛBƧ ΛND ƧTEREOTYPEƧ ◙

Purposes

1. To recognize popular stereotypes of Arabs
2. To discover Arabian stereotypes of the United States
3. To recognize how those stereotypes affect intercultural communication

> NOTE: If your native country is not the United States, consider the ethnocentric judgments that occur between your country and the people of the Arab states.

Instructions

1. Whether or not you are a member of the group, identify commonly held stereotypes of Arabs and stereotypes that Arabs may have of the United States.
2. Give the sources of those stereotypes.
3. Explain how those stereotypes affect intercultural communication.

Stereotypes About Arabs	*Source*	*Effect*
Example: Religious fanatics devoted to a nonwestern warrior religion	Popular movies Popular press	Believe they are blind to reason

Stereotypes About the United States	*Source*	*Effect*
Example: People are sex maniacs— everything revolves around sex.	Popular movies Popular behavior	Distrust

MORE

Conclusions

1. What have been the major sources of the stereotypes?

2. How have the stereotypes affected intercultural communication?

EXERCISE 4.5: STEREOTYPES AND PREJUDICE ON CAMPUS

Purposes

1. To recognize stereotyping and prejudice on campus
2. To analyze the effects of stereotyping and prejudice on campus
3. To consider ways of responding to stereotyping and prejudice

Instructions

Recall an incident of spoken or nonverbal stereotyping or prejudice that happened on your campus. It may be something that happened to you or something that you witnessed. Describe the incident in the space below.

Conclusions

1. What effects do you think the stereotype or prejudice had on the person or group that was the intended receiver?

2. In your opinion, what effects did communicating the stereotype or prejudice have on the source?

3. What effects do you think the stereotype or prejudice had on other people who overheard the message?

4. What are some ways that the person or group that was the intended receiver and those who overheard the message could respond?

CHAPTER 5

Nonverbal Communication

When we learn to communicate, we learn not only a spoken language but also the various other ways that people communicate meaning within our culture. Communicators use both verbal and nonverbal modes to communicate, and listeners expect to receive both kinds of messages during a conversation. If a speaker uses nonverbal codes poorly or inappropriately, a listener may consider the person a poor speaker. Because speakers and listeners expect nonverbal codes they both know, misunderstandings can occur when the speakers and listeners are from different cultures that generally do not share the same nonverbal codes.

Nonverbal communication codes can be divided into different types.

Proxemics is the way we use fixed space and personal space. Cultures vary in such things as how living space is arranged and how close to stand together.

Kinesics are behaviors like gestures, body movements, facial expressions, and eye contact. Certain facial expressions like smiles are universal, but many gestures are not. What may be an innocent gesture in one culture may be insulting in another.

Chronemics is how we perceive and use time. Chronemics also includes ideas about politeness that are related to time, such as whether or not you can be late for an appointment.

Paralanguage refers to sounds and other nonverbal elements that can be produced by the mouth and voice. Sounds like laughter or "uh,", "um," and "psst," how loudly or softly we speak, how high or low we speak, and how long or short we say vowel sounds in words are all examples of paralanguage. Paralanguage can change the meaning of what we say. Consider the polite expression, "Excuse me." Depending on how it is said, its meaning can range from a polite apology to an insulting exclamation.

Silence can be used to communicate a lot of different meanings that often depend on culture. In general, Eastern cultures value silence more than Western cultures do. In the United States, silence is often seen negatively. If a person is silent, many people think that the person is not paying attention or is not interested. Many U.S. citizens feel uncomfortable during extended periods of silence, and they often try to "fill" the silence by talking.

Haptics is communicating by touch. Touch can communicate a wide variety of messages. The meaning of touch depends on the kind of touch (hard, gentle, etc.) and the context. Different societies have different norms for touching. These rules determine the kinds of touching that are appropriate for certain situations and social relationships.

Clothing obviously can communicate meaning. What we wear commonly communicates information such as group or subgroup membership and marital status. The significance of certain articles of clothing and the symbols that may be used in clothing are unique to each culture.

Territoriality refers to how space can be used to communicate. For example, physical space, such a home, office, or public area, can be arranged to encourage conversation. Feng shui is the Chinese art of placement to create a balanced environment in a building, home, or office.

Olfactics is communicating by smell. Many companies, for example, use scents to advertise their products. Cultures have different opinions about what smells good or bad. People in the United States do not like the body's natural smell, so they bathe often and wear fragrances that cover up this odor.

Oculesics is communicating with the eyes. What the eyes communicate often depends on the culture. In the United States, it is usual for people to maintain eye contact. If a person tries to avoid eye contact in a conversation, the other person may think that person is dishonest. In some Asian cultures like Japan, students will often avoid making eye contact with their instructors as a sign of respect.

It is important to remember that all cultures do not share the same nonverbal behaviors or the same interpretation of them. Although crying is a nonverbal behavior that exists in many cultures, each culture may have different rules about it, such as when and where it is appropriate and who may do it. For example, in a society that has the norm "men do not cry," a man who cries may be considered emotionally weak.

## EXERCISE 5.1: OBSERVATIONS OF NONVERBAL COMMUNICATION 	◙

Purposes

1. To recognize and categorize nonverbal behaviors
2. To recognize that the meanings of nonverbal behaviors are subjective

Instructions

1. With at least one other person observe a group of two or three people having a conversation in a public place. From a distance and out of hearing range, observe this group for 15 to 20 minutes. Without comparing notes during the observation, note the nonverbal behaviors that you observe and later indicate what you believed was being communicated by the different behaviors.

2. Compare your observations and conclusions with those of your partner(s) and discuss any differences.

Behavior Description	Nonverbal Type	Communication Message
Example: One touched other's arm	Haptics	Emphasize point being made verbally

Conclusions

What can you conclude about the comparison of your observation with that of your partner(s)?

▣   **EXERCISE 5.2: LIVING SPACE AND
NONVERBAL COMMUNICATION**

Purpose

To recognize how the physical environment affects communication

Instructions

1. Draw a floor plan of your current place of residence. Also include major pieces of furniture in your plan.

2. Label the typical conversation patterns attached to specific areas of your home (i.e., light conversation over dinner table, intimate conversation in bedroom, etc.).

Conclusions

1. How are shelter environment and communication related?

2. How are privacy and roles reflected in the environment?

3. How do you think your floor plan and conversation patterns might change if your residence were in a very hot and/or cold climate?

▣ **EXERCISE 5.3: SYMBOLS**

Purpose

To associate symbols with the group most likely to recognize them

Instructions

The happy yellow smiley face is a symbol created in the 1960s as an employee morale booster and seems to appear everywhere, even on a 1999 U.S. postal stamp. In e-mail, smiley appears as a colon, hyphen, and parenthesis :-). Reproduce commonly used symbols associated with the following:

1. Religious symbols (Religious symbols date to prehistoric times.)

2. Other widely recognized symbols

3. Symbols found only in particular regions, states, or cities in the United States

4. Symbols more familiar to certain ethnic groups, such as trademarks for brands of ethnic foods

5. Symbols of colleges and universities, airlines, buses, trains, hotels, cars, clothing, chinaware, etc. (for example, Nike's "swoosh" symbol)

6. Symbols more easily recognized by most men or most women

EXERCIƧE 5.4: MARKING TIME ▣

Purpose

To learn to convert local time into time in other time zones

Instructions

Part 1

Before modern communication and transportation systems, problems of time differences from one location to another were minimal. But with the development of the telegraph and railroad, the need for a uniform time system became apparent. In the United States in the 1870s, over 50 different time zones were developed and used by different railroad companies. If a city was served by different railroad companies, that city might have different times according to each railroad. To solve this problem, the U.S. railroads had by 1883 adopted a system of four time zones.

In 1884, the United States hosted an international conference that developed today's worldwide system of time zones. The basis for time zones is that the earth is divided into 24 time zones equal to 15 degrees of longitude. The meridian that passes through Greenwich, England, was assigned a meridian of 0° longitude; 7.5° to either side of that line comprises the Greenwich mean time zone (also known as "Zero time," or "Z-time," or "Zulu time"). France initially objected to using "British" time and tried to initiate "Paris Mean Time." Successive zones to the east of the Greenwich zone are ahead of Greenwich time by 1 hour for each 15 degrees. Thus the reading "longitude 45° E" means that it is 3 hours ahead of Greenwich time, so that when it is noon at Greenwich, it is 3 p.m. at longitude 45° East. Each zone to the west of Greenwich is 1 hour behind Greenwich time for each 15 degrees of longitude.

The International Date Line is an imaginary line through the Pacific Ocean and roughly corresponds to 180° longitude. To the east of this line, the calendar date is one day earlier than to the west.

A few countries continue to use local time only. The whole of China, which extends through 50 degrees of longitude, uses only a single time. Nonetheless, the system of time zones shows the effect of modern communication and transportation systems on time.

1. Write down the current day of the week and time in standard time (not daylight savings time) for your location.

Your Day and Time: _____

2. Then, using the table below, calculate the day and time for the locations shown.

Country	Hours From GMT	Time at 1200 Hours GMT

Current day and time in:

Germany	+1	1300
Japan	+9	2100
Singapore	+8	2000
Turkey	+3	1500
United Kingdom	0	1200
United States, Eastern	−5	0700
United States, Hawaii	−10	0200

Istanbul

London

Munich

Singapore

Tokyo

Part 2

Counting years from the birth of Jesus was proposed in the 6th century and first became general in the Western church after the 9th century. With the papal jubilee in the year 1300, Europeans began to think in centuries.

Year: 20__

Year according to the Jewish calendar   _____

Year according to the Moslem calendar: _____

Year according to the Buddhist calendar: _____

Year in the current Maya great cycle: _____

According to the Chinese calendar year of the: _____

Purpose

To recognize cultural influences on clothing

Instructions

Describe clothing that is unique to a culture, subculture, or subgroup.

Conclusions

Explain how that clothing reflects elements of the culture, subculture, or subgroup.

▣ **EXERCISE 5.6: CULTURE AND EMOTIONS**

Purpose

To recognize how culture affects the expression and interpretation of emotions

Instructions

It is said that because of a homogeneous cooperative culture, Japanese people traditionally tend to avoid conflict. Most disputes are resolved through discussion. A person who expresses emotions first is regarded as the loser. For example, a police officer at an accident scene may perceive the emotionally expressive person as guilty. For each of the situations below describe how people from each country might interpret an emotion from the behavior described.

Behavior/Event	Japanese Interpretation of Emotion	U.S. Interpretation of Emotion
Example: Accident victim crying while testifying in court	Lacks calmness	Favorably impressed
Interaction between drivers of two cars involved in an accident		
Political candidate losing composure in public		
Sports team winning an important game		
Salesperson losing an important contract		

Conclusions

1. In what ways does culture affect the expression of emotions?

2. In what ways does one's culture affect the interpretation of the behaviors, emotions, or lack of emotions of someone from a different culture?

CHAPTER 6

Knowing Culture Through Language

The idea that culture and language are connected may not be obvious at first. When we learned our native language, we also unconsciously learned our culture. However, if a person learns another language or grows up speaking more than one language, the person may become aware of the different ways that each language allows a speaker to perceive and describe reality. These differences in perception are differences in culture. So the relationship between language and culture is that they are like mirrors to each other. Each one reflects and is reflected by the other.

Linguists have studied the relationship between language and culture, and it is described in the Sapir-Whorf hypothesis. This theory says that cultural elements can be seen in the vocabulary and grammar of a language. If a language has a rich vocabulary for certain things or ideas, it is easy to describe those things or ideas in that language. If the language makes it easy to express such things or ideas, they must be important to the culture. A similar relationship exists between the grammar of a language and a culture. Grammar allows the expression of ideas such as time and mood. If the grammar of a language does not allow a speaker to describe certain relationships, either that culture must not perceive them or does not consider them important.

Linguists have also studied the relationship that languages have to each other, noting that languages constantly change and that words have an arbitrary relationship to what they represent. Using these assumptions, they have searched for the "mother tongue" for all of the modern languages. So far they have been able to divide languages into families that are based on a certain resemblance to each other. Three such families are Indo-European, Altaic, and Nostratic. It is believed that language originated first in Africa.

Although spoken languages have existed for about 100,000 years, written language developed about 5,000 years ago. The first writing was cuneiform, which was a pictographic form of writing. Pictograms represent ideas, whereas phonetic forms of writing represent sounds.

When cultures have contact but share no common language, a number of things may occur. First, a pidgin may develop. A pidgin is a trade language that has elements of the dominant language or languages, but with a greatly reduced vocabulary and grammar. Pidgins have no native speakers. Second, a creole may develop. Creoles are pidgins that have become "nativized." They have native speakers, and their vocabulary and grammar are expanded to the point of being complete languages. A third possibility is that the cultures will simply choose a language to use for communication purposes. In modern times, one of the most commonly chosen languages for this purpose is English. An artificial language, Esperanto, was developed as a universal second language, but its use is not widespread.

◙ **EXERCISE 6.1: BRITISH, AUSTRALIAN, NEW ZEALAND, AND AMERICAN ENGLISH**

Purpose

To recognize differences between English spoken in the United States and that spoken in Great Britain

Instructions

Part 1

Match the British word to its U.S. equivalent.

British English	American English
____ 1. biscuit	a. bathroom
____ 2. booking clerk	b. bus
____ 3. boot	c. candy
____ 4. charwoman	d. canned meat
____ 5. chemist	e. chips
____ 6. chips	f. cleaning lady
____ 7. climbing frame	g. cookie
____ 8. coach	h. crosswalk
____ 9. commercial bagman	i. dessert
____ 10. crisps	j. elevator
____ 11. dustman	k. eraser
____ 12. French bean	l. flashlight
____ 13. ice lolly	m. French fries
____ 14. joint	n. garbage collector
____ 15. jumper	o. jungle gym
____ 16. knickers	p. mail
____ 17. knock me up	q. pharmacist
____ 18. ladder	r. popsicle
____ 19. lift	s. pullover sweater
____ 20. loo	t. raisin
____ 21. lorry	u. rare
____ 22. naughts and crosses	v. roast
____ 23. pavement	w. run in stocking
____ 24. post	x. sidewalk
____ 25. pudding	y. spool of thread
____ 26. reel of cotton	z. string bean
____ 27. rubber	aa. tenderloin
____ 28. sultana	bb. ticket agent
____ 29. sweet	cc. tic-tac-toe
____ 30. tinned meat	dd. traveling salesperson
____ 31. torch	ee. truck
____ 32. undercut	ff. trunk of car
____ 33. underdone	gg. underpants
____ 34. vest	hh. undershirt
____ 35. zebra crossing	ii. wake me up

Part 2

Match the Australian (A) and/or New Zealand (NZ) word to its U.S. equivalent.

Australian/New Zealand English	*American English Equivalent*
_____ 1. barbie (A)	a. a country person (someone from the bush)
_____ 2. bung on (A)	b. a living or job
_____ 3. bushie (A)	c. appetizer
_____ 4. crust (A)	d. auto bodywork repairer
_____ 5. dairy (NZ)	e. barbeque
_____ 6. entree (NZ)	f. convenience store
_____ 7. garbo (A)	g. gelatin dessert (jello)
_____ 8. jelly (A, NZ)	h. pullover
_____ 9. jersey (NZ)	i. someone from New Zealand
_____ 10. kiwi (A, NZ)	j. someone who collects garbage
_____ 11. panel beater (A, NZ)	k. to stage or orchestrate something
_____ 12. sheila (A)	l. woman

Compare your answers to those in the Answers section at the end of the workbook.

▣ **EXERCISE 6.2: AMERICAN ENGLISH BORROWINGS**

Purpose

To recognize how American English borrowing reflects contacts between cultures

Instructions

English is a mixture of many languages. Words borrowed long ago are now considered part of the language. Use a dictionary such as the *American Heritage Dictionary of the English Language* to determine the origin of the following "English" words and speculate the era or circumstances when the word entered the English language:

Group 1

1. moccasin
2. opossum
3. raccoon

Group 2

1. bayou
2. butte
3. prairie

Group 3

1. mustang
2. poncho
3. rodeo

Group 4

1. coleslaw
2. cookies
3. waffles

Group 5

1. gumbo
2. hip
3. jazz

EXERCISE 6.3: TRANSLATING PIDGINS ◙

Purpose

To recognize how pidgin languages facilitate communication between cultures

Instructions

Match the following words from pidgin developed in New Guinea to their English equivalents

Part 1

_____ 1. bagarap
_____ 2. daunim koldies
_____ 3. fols tits
_____ 4. gavmen
_____ 5. glas bilong lukluk
_____ 6. hariap
_____ 7. haus lotu bilong ol mahomet
_____ 8. haus sick
_____ 9. klostu
_____ 10. lusim
_____ 11. man bilong bigmaus
_____ 12. marys
_____ 13. niuspepa
_____ 14. pen bilong maus
_____ 15. pidgin
_____ 16. pikininis
_____ 17. piksa bilong bigpela man
_____ 18. pipols
_____ 19. plis
_____ 20. sarap
_____ 21. tankyu
_____ 22. tok gude
_____ 23. tumora
_____ 24. yesa

a. abandon
b. adults-only film
c. agree
d. almost
e. business
f. children
g. drink cold beer
h. false teeth
i. government
j. greet
k. hospital
l. hurry up
m. lipstick
n. loudmouth
o. mess up (or bugger up in Australian English)
p. mirror
q. mosque
r. newspaper
s. people
t. please
u. shut up
v. thank you
w. tomorrow
x. women

MORE

Part 2

_____	1. All pau	a.	Are you going to be there if I go?
_____	2. Ats why hard	b.	Better
_____	3. Boddah you?	c.	Come here
_____	4. Bruddah	d.	Delicious
_____	5. Bulae	e.	Does that bother you?
_____	7. Da kine	f.	Don't exaggerate or don't pretend
_____	6. Bum bye	g.	Finished or it's over
_____	8. Howzit, brah?	h.	How are you, friend?
_____	9. Less go kau kau	i.	Later
_____	10. Lolo	j.	Let's eat
_____	11. Mo bettah	k.	Male friend
_____	12. Moke	l.	Stupid
_____	13. No ack	m.	That's life

Compare your answers to those in the Answers section at the end of the workbook.

Conclusions

1. What conclusions can you reach about pidgins?

2. How can the use of pidgins be a basis for prejudice?

Purpose

To become familiar with the universal language Esperanto

Instructions

Attempt to read and translate the following paragraph written in Esperanto. Compare your results with others.

La inteligenta persono lernas la interlingvon Esperanto rapide kaj facile. Esperanto estas la moderna, kultura lingvo por la internacia mondo. Simpla, flekselbla, praktika solvo de la problemo de universala interkompreno, Esperanto meritas vian seriozan konsideron. Lernu la interlingvon Esperanto!

Conclusions

1. Did others find the translation easier or harder than you? Why?

2. What made Esperanto easy to translate?

◙ **EXERCISE 6.5: WRITE A HAIKU**

The haiku is a traditional form of Japanese lyric poetry. It is written in three lines of 5-7-5 syllables. The subject matter of haiku is typically nature. If written in the traditional manner, a haiku will contain one word that refers to a season either directly or symbolically. The following haiku was written by Basho:

Uguisu ya	A warbler
Take no ko-yabu ni	In the grove of bamboo shoots
Oi o naku	Growing old, sings.

Japanese men and women of all ages and circumstances traditionally marked various junctures in their lives by creating haiku to express their personal feelings. Many people memorized haiku poems for enjoyment. In the 18th century, *ren*, or social gatherings for the sole purpose of creating poetry, spread throughout Japanese society.

Purpose

To appreciate how a culture's poetic form can reflect other aspects of that culture

Instructions

Write a haiku.

Conclusions

1. What caused you the most difficulty when you wrote your haiku?

2. The form of the haiku is very brief, but it conveys a lot of meaning. What conclusions can you make about Japanese language and culture?

3. How does the subject matter of the haiku compare to the subject matter of the poetry of your country?

CHAPTER 7

Language as a Barrier

Language can be defined as the set of symbols shared by a community to communicate meaning and experience. Unique aspects of cultures are reflected in the languages spoken by their populations. Language can become a barrier to communication when these unique aspects interfere with translation. It can also become a barrier when a group of people is forced to speak a language it does not want to.

Five elements that typically cause problems in translation are the lack of equivalences in vocabulary, idioms, grammar and syntax, experiences, and concepts. Sometimes, translations cannot be made on a word-for-word basis because words that exist in one language may not exist in another. Idioms present a similar problem in that they, too, cannot be translated word for word. The words that make up an idiomatic expression normally do not make sense at a literal level. Languages also do not all share the same grammar and syntax. Translations that have incorrect grammar and syntax can be confusing or even change the meaning from what was originally intended. Cultures often do not share the same experiences. Translation becomes problematic when one culture has certain experiences and another does not. Last, cultures may not understand concepts in the same way. Concepts like "equality" and "freedom" mean different things in different cultures. One way to avoid translation problems is to "back translate," which is to first translate the concept into one language and then translate it back into the original language. Doing so makes it possible to check a translation for accuracy.

Language can be a barrier when it becomes an issue of nationalism. Because language carries elements of culture, many countries fear the influence on their own culture that the introduction of a new language may have. One response to this concern is to limit the influence of nondominant languages within a country. Examples of this type of action are the "English only" movement in the United States and the French Academy's efforts to keep the French language pure of foreign words. National bilingualism can also have certain problems, as the separatist movement in Canada shows. One negative effect of language nationalism is the loss of language and culture of nondominant groups within a country.

EXERCISE 7.1: EXPLAINING IDIOMS ▣

Purpose

1. To recognize idioms in English and other languages
2. To explain the meanings of common idioms

Instructions

Every language has idioms. Idioms are expressions that do not make sense on a literal level. Native speakers of a language usually do not think about the meaning of the individual words that make up the expression. Instead, they only pay attention to the meaning of the expression as a whole. Idioms are difficult for people learning a new language because, even if they understand the words, they do not know what the phrase means.

1. Make a list of common English idioms.

2. "Translate" the idiom into what it actually means (the figurative meaning of the phrase, not the literal meanings of the words).

3. Try to find idioms in other languages as well. For these, write down the literal meaning of the words and the figurative meaning of the phrase.

English Idioms	Meaning
Examples:	
Pushing up daisies	Dead
I wasn't born yesterday.	I am not stupid (or naive).

Other Idioms	Meaning
Me costó un ojo de la cara (Spanish)	Literally "it cost me an eye from from my face" (compare to "it cost me an arm and a leg"), it was expensive
Il est bête comme ses pieds (French)	Literally "he is dumb like his feet," he is stupid

◙ **EXERCISE 7.2: SPREAD OF ENGLISH INTO OTHER LANGUAGES**

Purpose

To appreciate how English is used in other languages

Instructions

Match the following borrowed words to their English language equivalent.

_____	1. biznessmyen (Russian)	a.	"bucks" or dollars
_____	2. bakks (Russian)	b.	businessmen
_____	3. el ampayer (Spanish)	c.	chewing gum
_____	4. futbol (Russian)	d.	cocktail
_____	5. gamberger (Russian)	e.	coffee
_____	6. gamu (Japanese)	f.	football
_____	7. garu-furendo (Japanese)	g.	girlfriend
_____	8. herkot (Ukrainian)	h.	haircut
_____	9. hitchhiken (German)	i.	hamburger
_____	10. jiipu (Japanese)	j.	homerun hitters
_____	11. koohii (Japanese)	k.	jeeps
_____	12. le coquetel (French)	l.	mass communication
_____	13. le pique-nique (French)	m.	moving pictures
_____	14. los jonroneros (Spanish)	n.	personal computer
_____	15. masu-komi (Japanese)	o.	picnic
_____	16. muving pikceris (Polish)	p.	sweater
_____	17. parken (German)	q.	hitchhike
_____	18. pasocon (Japanese)	r.	to park
_____	19. suéter (Spanish)	s.	umpire
_____	20. verd protsesser (Russian)	t.	word processor

Check your answers against those in the Answers section at the back of the workbook.

CHAPTER 8

Culture's Influence on Perception

In the past few years in the United States, "magic eye" pictures have become popular. These pictures at first seem to be just a lot of wavy lines. However, if they are looked at in the right way, a hidden picture can be seen. Some people can see the hidden image right away; others take much longer. A few frustrated people never learn to see them. Even though everyone who looks at them sees the same thing (i.e., wavy lines hiding a picture), there are differences in what they perceive (i.e., wavy lines or a picture). In a similar way, cultures affect how people perceive the world. Everyone is able to sense the world in the same way, but cultures teach us how to process and understand the information obtained from our senses.

The information received about the world comes through our physical senses of sight, sound, smell, taste, and touch. Our sense of touch also allows us to feel pressure, temperature, and pain. Imagine how our perceptions might change if we had more acute senses or another kind of sense such as a dolphin's ability to use sonar.

To some degree, cultures affect what people sense, but they have a much greater influence on perceptions. The process of perception can be divided into three stages: selection, organization, and interpretation. In the selection stage, we choose what sensory information to pay attention to. Our senses constantly provide us with an enormous amount of information. We cannot be consciously aware of it all. Therefore, we must choose only the most relevant information for us. Our cultures teach us what is relevant. For example, we pay close attention to the sounds of our native language, but it is more difficult for us to hear and tell the difference between the sounds of foreign languages. Organization is the second stage of the perception process. When we organize information, we place it into categories. Some cultures may categorize certain things in great detail; others might not. The Eskimo culture, for example, has many categories for snow. Interpretation is the third stage in the perception process. In this stage, we give meaning to or "decode" the information that we have selected and organized. People can interpret the same information in completely different ways. A classic example is the 8-oz. glass with 4 ounces of water in it. Is it half empty or half full?

Cultural differences in interpretation can be quite dramatic, as in the case of food. What one culture enjoys eating, another culture may find disgusting. It is important to remember that food choice and preparation can be understood in relation to other aspects of culture. The physical geography of a country has a strong effect on culture. It influences clothing, housing, and food. Japanese people, for example, live on a group of islands and consequently eat a lot of fish because it is a food source that is easily available. North Americans eat a lot of beef because the United States has plenty of land on which to graze cattle.

▣ EXERCISE 8.1: COMPARING SENSATION

Purpose

To discover how sense organs define the world

Instructions

1. Use an encyclopedia or other reference source to learn the ways that different forms of life sense the world and the limits to these senses.
2. Use that information to speculate as to how each form of life experiences the external world.

Life Form	Senses	Experience of World
Example: Dogs	Poor sight, no color vision Acute hearing and smell senses	A world of smells and sounds
Bees		
Fish		
Frogs		
Whales		
Worms		

Conclusions

What can be concluded about the reality of the external world?

EXERCISE 8.2: OBSERVATION AND INTERPRETATION

Purpose

To recognize how differing interpretations can be assigned to the same observation

Instructions

1. Make a list of observations about life in the United States.
2. Come up with two differing interpretations that could each be logical for this observation.

Observations	Interpretation #1	Interpretation #2
Example: People are always going somewhere	Busy, industrious people	Do not appreciate the present

Conclusions

How do these interpretations affect communication?

◙   **EXERCISE 8.3: FOOD PREJUDICES**

Purpose

To investigate your own food prejudices

Instructions

1. Make a list of exotic food you enjoy.
2. Think about when you learned to enjoy it.
3. Now list foods that you may be unwilling to try.
4. What reasons do you have for not wanting to try them?

Exotic Food Enjoyed	Circumstances
Example: calamari (squid)	Grandmother served to whole family on special occasions—included in category of "foods associated with family"

Exotic Food Unwilling to Try	Reasons
Example: snails	Perceive them in category of "garden pests"

Purpose

To recognize how words and labels influence perception

Instructions

1. Choose a partner who is about the same size as you. Stand about 5 feet apart and face each other.

2. Look at your partner for about 30-45 seconds and think of all the words you can to describe that person. Try to observe every little detail about the person (face, eyes, hair, clothes, fingernails, etc.).

3. Keep the same partner and observe the person again (for about 30 seconds). However, do this without words. Do not attempt to describe what you see. Simply observe the essence of what is in front of you.

Conclusions

1. Compare how you felt when your partner observed you the first time and the second time.

2. Compare how it felt to observe the first and second time.

3. When you were looking at your partner for the first time, what kind of words did you use to describe that person (generally speaking—don't list the words)?

4. Consider how descriptive words or labels affect your perceptions and expectations of people. Comment on this relationship.

CHAPTER 9

Dimensions of Culture

How tall are you? How much do you weigh? Whatever you answer, you will be using some kind of measurement to describe these characteristics about yourself. We often use measurements to compare things. For example, if we want to know if one room is bigger than another one, we measure its length and width to find out. These measurements are called dimensions. In a similar way, cultures can be compared by measuring their dimensions. However, the dimensions used to compare cultures are generally not physical measurements but, instead, are measures of the values and attitudes that different cultures have. These are called value dimensions.

Geert Hofstede originally identified four dimensions of culture: individualism (versus collectivism), masculinity (versus femininity), power distance, and uncertainty avoidance. Individualistic cultures give more importance to individuals' needs when they do things such as setting goals. Collectivist cultures, on the other hand, give more importance to the needs of the group. The masculinity-femininity dimension measures a culture's dominant values ranging from aggressive (masculine trait) to nurturing (feminine trait). Also, masculine cultures generally keep masculine and feminine behaviors separate and value assertiveness, competition, and material wealth. Feminine cultures may have overlapping gender roles and focus on quality of life, interpersonal relationships, and concern for the weak. Power distance describes the distribution of influence within the culture. Is power held by just a few people, or is it held by many? Uncertainty avoidance measures how much ambiguity people will endure and how much risk they like to take. Cultures that are high in uncertainty avoidance are aggressive, emotional, compulsive, and intolerant, whereas cultures that are low in uncertainty avoidance are thoughtful, relaxed, less aggressive, accepting of risks, and generally tolerant.

There are other value dimensions besides the four mentioned above. One of these is called Confucian work dynamism, now called long-term versus short-term orientation. The Confucian dynamism dimension emphasizes thrift (spending money wisely), persistence and hard work, having a sense of shame, and ordering relationships (i.e., a system for giving certain relationships more or less importance). Singapore is a country with high Confucian work dynamism. Other dimensions measure a culture's use of nonverbal behavior. These dimensions are high versus low context and immediacy and expressiveness. Cultures with high context generally use fewer words to communicate and rely on shared cultural experience to communicate their meaning. Low-context cultures rely more on words to communicate meaning. The United States is a low-context culture. Immediacy and expressiveness refer to the way that cultures express "warmth" and "closeness." Examples of immediacy behaviors are touching, eye contact, smiling, and maintaining close physical distance. Arabian cultures are high in immediacy behaviors.

▣ EXERCISE 9.1: HOW NONVERBALS REFLECT CULTURAL DIMENSIONS

Purpose

To recognize how nonverbals reflect cultural dimensions

Instructions

For each cultural dimension, describe the nonverbal that would correspond to that dimension.

Cultural Dimension	Expected Nonverbals
Immediacy and expressiveness	Example: Frequent hugs, standing close together
Individualism	
Collectivism	
Masculinity	
Femininity	
High power distance	
Low power distance	
High uncertainty avoidance	
Low uncertainty avoidance	
Long-term orientation	
Short-term orientation	
High context	
Low context	

EXERCISE 9.2: CHILDREN'S STORIES AND CULTURAL DIMENSIONS   ▣

Purpose

To discover cultural dimensions in children's stories

Instructions

Many children's stories transcend cultural boundaries with universal themes, while others reflect a culture's unique cultural dimensions. First, find a children's story that can be clearly identified with one culture. Examples include "The Little Engine That Could" from the United States and "Peach Boy" from Japan. Summarize the story below. Then, identify the cultural dimensions reflected in the story.

STORY TITLE: _____

ORIGIN: _____

Summary

Cultural Dimensions in Story

Conclusions

How do the values in the story relate to past and current dominant culture values?

▣ **EXERCISE 9.3: INTERVIEWING INTERNATIONAL STUDENTS ON CULTURE**

Purpose

To learn about the home culture of an international student studying in the United States

Instructions

Interview an international student on the student's home culture. Use the following suggestions to help you do the interview:

1. To make the student feel more comfortable, ask about the student's first childhood memory. You should begin first by talking about one of your own memories. Compare the two early memories from you and the student. Consider how each of them reflects each of your cultures.

2. Ask about the country itself: history, geography, government, and transportation and education systems.

3. Ask about the people: language, religion, family customs, diet, recreation, and work.

4. Ask about communication: important words and phrases, gestures and clothing, and newspaper, radio, and television systems. You may ask the student to talk about differences (grammar, ways of saying things) between English and the student's native language (recall the Sapir-Whorf hypothesis).

Conclusions

From this interview, what can you conclude about values important in this person's home culture?

Purpose

To gain insights into Japanese culture through its proverbs

Instructions

Proverbs are epigrammatic sayings that express common concerns. Proverbs say what a people think are important in ways that people can remember. Many *kotowaza* (Japanese proverbs) originated in China; some are more recent Western borrowings. But whatever their origin, they say something about Japanese life. What do the following Japanese proverbs say about Japanese life?

Approximate English equivalents are shown in the Answers section at the back of the workbook.

1. Deru kugi wa utareru. (The protruding nail will be hammered.)

2. Issun no mushi ni mo go-bu no tamashii. (Even a one-inch insect has a half-inch soul.)

3. Kuni horobite sanga ari. (Destroy a country, but its mountains and rivers remain.)

4. Saru mo ki kara ochiru. (Even monkeys fall from trees.)

MORE ▶

5. Shitashiki naka ni mo reigi ari. (There are formalities between the closest of friends.)

6. Kuchi wa wazawai no moto. (The mouth is the cause of calamity.)

7. Kusai mono ni futa. (Put or putting a lid on what smells bad.)

8. Ko wa sangai no kubikase. (Children yoke parents to the past, present, and future.)

Conclusions

How do these proverbs reflect Japanese life in the past and in the present?

SOURCE: David Galef, *"Even Monkeys Fall From Trees" and Other Japanese Proverbs* (Rutland, VT/Tokyo, Japan: Charles E. Tuttle, 1987).

EXERCISE 9.5: USING NEW CULTURAL KNOWLEDGE: JAPAN   ◙

Purpose

To use knowledge of the Japanese culture to examine intercultural communication situations

Instructions

Read and analyze the e-mail message below reprinted exactly as received. Consider such things as what cultural values are being reflected and how the incident could have been avoided or handled differently.

> To: fjandt@mail.csusb.edu
> From: Shiro
> Subject: Problem About Communication Class
> Dear Fred E. Jandt,
>
> I'm writing to you and your capacity as spiritual adviser to ask for wise suggestion(s) for improving my group session in the Communication class.
>   The problem in my team is that another member except me seems to discuss without me because I think my English is so limited. Actually, I came from Okinawa, Japan, and I've been Seattle for 1 year. Now, our Communication class has started since this winter quarter, and we've read Intercultural Communication which was written by you. As we've learned from your text book so far, it seems to me we couldn't communicate each other. I confirmed it's my fault party, but not whole. I need more effort to improve my English, however, their attitudes toward me is also problem. It seems to me that they don't care about me, just care about their grade. In the last group assignment, our group got lower score. One of member was really upset, and his attitude implied because of my fault. Even though I told them please help me at the first session, they have never helped me. They just talked each other, and I just felt like audience.
>   I don't want to blame my instructor and even my classmates, so I want to improve this situation by myself with your advice. I don't want to quit this class because I like to study Communication.
>   I'm wondering if you could have some spare time to give me some tips on this problem. I will be grateful for any advice you can give me. I truly need your words of wisdom.
>   I'm looking forward to your excellent advice on this matter. Thank you very much.
>
> Shiro

SOURCE: Reprinted with the permission of the writer.

CHAPTER 10

Dominant United States Cultural Patterns: Using Value Orientation Theory

Although human beings live in different geographic areas, speak different languages, and wear different kinds of clothes, everyone shares the same basic problems. Every culture deals with these universal problems in a unique way and has its own philosophy about them. The problems that all cultures face are the relationship between humans and nature (man-nature orientation), how we engage in our daily activities (activity orientation), how we use and perceive time (temporal orientation), questions about our own nature (human-nature orientation), and the relationship between an individual and other people (relational).

Human-nature orientation can also be called "worldview" and describes how people view their relation to nature. Do they see themselves as superior to nature and try to control it? Do they try to work in harmony with nature? Or are they the victims of nature? Activity orientation describes how people do, don't do, or change things. In other words, people either passively accept events, change events that are already happening, or initiate events on their own. Time orientation describes how people in a culture focus more on the past, present, or future. Human-nature orientation relates to a culture's beliefs about humans being naturally good, bad, or both. Relational orientation looks at how cultures organize relationships between people. Is it based on a hierarchy, on group identification, or on individualism?

By using the five value orientation categories, it is possible to describe the cultural patterns of a country. The United States may be becoming more regionalized; that is, its cultural patterns may be a little different in different parts of the country. However, some general observations can still be made. People in the United States generally believe in a supreme god or universal spirit and believe that they can control nature. They have a lot of faith in science and technology and are materialistic. They get a sense of identity from work and generally separate work from play. Americans are efficient, practical, and see progress and change as a good thing. They place a high value on time and have a future time orientation, although they often divide it into short-term goals.

People in the United States do not agree about whether humans are naturally good, bad, or a mixture of both. However, two beliefs related to human nature—rationality and mutability—are still believed by many Americans. Rationality is the belief that people are reasonable and can make decisions for themselves. Mutability is the belief that people can change. For example, a criminal can learn to be a good citizen. One of the most fundamental beliefs of people in the United States is individualism. Associated with this belief are the ideas of self-motivation, competition, and responsibility for one's own actions. Americans also have an unshakable belief in equality. They do not believe that everyone is the same, but they do believe that everyone does or should have the same opportunities as everyone else. This is the basis of the American Dream. Last, Americans are conformist—it is important to stay in touch with the latest fashions in hair, clothing, and so forth.

Purpose

To compare your own values to those identified as dominant United States cultural patterns

Instructions

Place a "+" in front of the statements you personally agree with, a "−" in front of those you believe are not true for you, and leave blank those with which you neither agree nor disagree.

_____   1. I believe in a personal God (i.e., a God I can know personally, like a friend)

_____   2. Human life is the most unique form of life.

_____   3. Humans have power to control the plants and animals of the earth.

_____   4. Science helps people.

_____   5. You can tell something about a person by their possessions.

_____   6. Buying things on credit (credit card, car loan, etc.) is okay.

_____   7. Work gives me a feeling of accomplishment.

_____   8. Work should be serious business.

_____   9. An active, busy life can be a satisfying life.

_____ 10. It's important to organize and plan your time.

_____ 11. It is more important to focus on achieving short-term goals than long-term goals because the distant future is uncertain.

_____ 12. Change is good.

_____ 13. New, improved products sell better than old ones.

_____ 14. Time should be managed responsibly.

_____ 15. We should use the present to work for a better future.

_____ 16. People are born with the potential for good and evil.

_____ 17. People can make decisions for themselves.

_____ 18. People can change their behavior.

_____ 19. It's important to have an identity that is based on yourself and not on other people.

_____ 20. It's important to decide goals for yourself.

_____ 21. Everyone should have equal opportunity.

_____ 22. It's fun to keep in touch with trends (e.g., fashion, hairstyles, and "cool" clubs).

_____ 23. I'm proud of my country.

_____ 24. I'm willing to fight for my country.

MORE

Conclusions

1. How do your values compare to the dominant United States cultural patterns?

2. Which three values on this list are the most important to you?

3. Can you identify when and where you first learned these three values?

4. Do these three values affect how you communicate? If so, how?

5. How do these three values affect your intercultural communication?

EXERCISE 10.2: DISCOVERING VALUES IN AXIOMS ◉

Purpose

To identify commonly held values in the United States

Instructions

1. Write down all the axioms, maxims, and proverbs that you have heard over and over again. These are the words of wisdom that your parents probably tried to tell you when you were growing up. Try to locate other sayings from different cultures.
2. Then determine what value is being taught.

Axiom	Value
Examples:	
The wheel that squeaks the loudest is the one that gets the grease.	Individualism (United States)
One arrow can be broken easily, but three arrows cannot be broken easily	Group orientation (Japan)

Conclusions

How do you believe axioms reflect and transmit cultural values?

SOURCE: Based on Robert Kohls, "A Way of Getting at American Values," in David S. Hoopes and Paul Ventura (Eds.), *Intercultural Sourcebook: Cross-Cultural Training Methodologies* (Chicago: Intercultural Press, 1979), p. 159.

CHAPTER 11

Comparative Cultural Patterns: Arabian Culture

The Western and Arabian cultures have much contact with each other, and misunderstandings occur between them. Intercultural communication barriers, especially stereotypes and insufficient knowledge of each other's cultures and languages, contribute to these continuing problems.

All the Arabian countries have a common language and religion. They are the Arabic language and the Islamic faith. The major difference between Western and Arabian culture is religion. The Islamic faith controls the lives of its members (called Muslims) in all areas of life. These areas include spiritual beliefs, lifestyle, laws, and government.

Arabian cultural patterns can be described by using the value orientation categories discussed in Chapter 10: worldview, activity orientation, time orientation, human-nature orientation, and relational orientation. Arabian cultural values are strongly influenced by the Islamic religion.

In Arabian worldview, everything in the world follows God's law perfectly, except for human beings who have the choice of whether or not to follow God's law. Arabian activity orientation encourages work and practicality. Progress and change, however, are accepted carefully because technology should not go against the teachings of the Koran (Islamic holy text). One important aspect of Arabian time orientation is the idea of polychronic time. Unlike monochronic cultures, polychronic cultures do many things at one time. In Arabian countries it is common for people to conduct business with many different people at the same time. Muslims view humans as basically good. People are born free of sin and become responsible for their actions when they grow up. Arabian relational orientation is based on the group, especially the family. People live in large extended families with a patriarch as family leader. What affects one member of the family affects the rest of the family. In Arabian culture, a woman's honor is protected by following strict clothing guidelines and by not interacting with males except for her husband or family members. Although there are many restrictions on women, they are viewed as equals to men.

Purposes

1. To recognize values that are not typical of the United States
2. To think about how different cultural values can affect intercultural communication

Instructions

1. Look at the list of cultural assumptions below. Choose one or more of these assumptions and then imagine what you think a culture would be like if it truly believed in those ideas. Write a description of the culture that you imagined.

2. Next, describe the kinds of intercultural communication problems that you think might happen between people from your imagined culture and your own (real) culture.

What would a society be like if it completely believed

1. in reincarnation and karma?
2. that people from other societies are infidels; that is, they are viewed with suspicion because they do not share the same religious beliefs?
3. that all events in the world are determined by fate or destiny?
4. what a person is worth (value to society) is determined solely by how well a person does what pleases them?
5. that it is better to live their lives passively instead of having an action orientation (i.e., allowing things to happen is better than trying to make things happen)?
6. that certain ethnic or racial groups are not as smart or emotionally mature as the regular members of the society are?
7. that old people should be respected, honored, and treated with deference in all instances?
8. that aesthetic values (ideas about beauty) are extremely important and should be used to determine every major issue in life?
9. that rights of groups are more important than an individual's rights?
10. that women are superior to men?

SOURCE: Based on Robert Kohls, " 'As If . . .' Exercise," in David S. Hoopes and Paul Ventura (Eds.), *Intercultural Sourcebook: Cross-Cultural Training Methodologies* (Chicago: Intercultural Press, 1979), p. 161.

▣   **EXERCISE 11.2: USING NEW CULTURAL KNOWLEDGE: ARABIAN CULTURE**

Purpose

To use knowledge of the Arabian culture to examine intercultural communication situations

Instructions

Read and analyze each of the incidents described below. Consider what cultural values are being reflected (both Saudi and American) and how the incident could have been avoided or handled differently.

1. An instructor gave a test to Saudi students. The test included information from the entire course. Two of the Saudis did very poorly; in fact, one student completely failed the test. When the instructor discussed the test results with them, they simply shrugged their shoulders and said, "Inshallah," which is an expression that means "It's in God's hands." The instructor replied, "But God didn't answer the test. You did!"

2. An Arab student worked as an assistant in a lab on campus. He asked his coworkers if they wanted to go to lunch with him at the Student Union. They agreed to go with him and said that it was time to eat. They all chatted together as they went to the Union, where they got in line at the cafeteria. When they reached the cashier's station, the Arab student, who was first in line, paid for all of them. When the group got to their table, his two coworkers insisted on giving the Arab student the money for their lunches. The Arab refused it, but the Americans insisted; and the coworker sitting beside him swept the money off the table and put it into the foreign student's jacket pocket. Afterward, the Americans were talking together and said that the Arab student had been unusually quiet and reserved while he ate his lunch.

3. Outside a classroom during a 10-minute break, several U.S. students and an Arab student were exchanging ideas about a project that they were working on together. At the beginning of the break, most of the Americans took out cigarettes and lit them. The Arab student watched them; then, hesitantly, he finally took out his own pack of cigarettes and lit one. After the break had ended and they returned to the classroom to work on their project, the Arab student was very quiet, and he seemed a little angry when he did speak.

SOURCE: Incidents adapted from *A Manual of Teaching Techniques for Intercultural Education* (Amherst: University of Massachusetts Press, 1971) and from Paula Barnak, "Critical Incidents Exercise," in David S. Hoopes and Paul Ventura (Eds.), *Intercultural Sourcebook: Cross-Cultural Training Methodologies* (Chicago: Intercultural Press, 1979), p. 134.

CHAPTER 12

Women, Families, and Children

Although the political and economic status of women is higher in some countries than in others, in all countries the status of women is lower than the status of men. It does not matter if a country is rich or poor; large differences between women's and men's status can occur in any country. Even though women and men do not have the same status, they are the most equal in the Nordic countries—Denmark, Finland, Norway, and Sweden—where women have a high rate of participation in government and their incomes are the closest to men's. In countries where there is a big difference in the economic status of women and men, there is often a noticeable lack of political participation and representation by women.

Girls and boys grow up in different worlds where they learn to communicate in different ways. For girls, language is for connection and intimacy. They play in small groups and share secrets. If a disagreement occurs while playing, girls typically stop the game and start a new one to avoid conflict. Boys, however, are taught that language is for getting and maintaining status and independence. They often play in larger groups and do team activities. When a disagreement occurs, boys typically stop the game and argue over the rules. In this way they compete for status and the ability to control the activities of other boys.

These two differing ideas of communication (language of connection or language of status) also are reflected in other aspects of women's and men's communication. For example, more women make suggestions, whereas more men give orders; more women use and accept touching more than most men do; and more women use conversation to create a feeling of connection, whereas most men give information. It is important to remember that these differences reflect only the average of all women and all men. In every culture, differences exist between women and men, and many of these differences are the result of cultural expectations and expected gender behavior. All people have similar potentials, but as we grow up we are taught gender roles that separate females from males and limit our potentials. For example, all people have the same potential for feeling emotions, but females are generally allowed to show a wider range of them. In modern times, the media have a strong influence on our images of women and men.

Purpose

To recognize how women and men communicate

Instructions

The 20 questions in this survey come from research that was done in U.S. classrooms, private homes, businesses, offices, and hospitals—the places where people commonly work and socialize. If you think that a statement correctly describes female or male communication patterns, mark it true. If you think that the statement does not correctly describe the communication pattern, mark it false. Compare your answers to those in the Answers section at the end of the workbook.

T F   1. Men talk more than women.

T F   2. It is more likely that a man will interrupt a woman than interrupt another man.

T F   3. The English language has approximately 10 times as many sexual terms for males as it does for females.

T F   4. During conversations, women spend more time looking at their partner than men do.

T F   5. Nonverbal messages have more meaning than verbal messages.

T F   6. When they communicate, female managers are more likely to show their feelings openly and be more dramatic than male managers.

T F   7. Men control the content of conversations, and they also work harder than women in keeping conversations going.

T F   8. When people hear words such as "mankind" and "he," they assume that the word means "females and males."

T F   9. Women are more likely to touch other people than men are.

T F 10. In classroom communications, teachers give more negative feedback (i.e., reprimands, criticism, scolding, etc.) to male students than to female students.

T F 11. Women are more likely than men to share very personal information (i.e., share secrets).

T F 12. Females speak in a more animated or excited style than males do.

T F 13. Women use less personal space than men do.

T F 14. When a male speaks, people pay more attention to him than they would to a female speaker, even when she says exactly the same thing as the man does.

T F 15. In general, women speak in a more tentative or uncertain style than men do.

T F 16. Women are more likely to answer questions that are intended for other people.

T F 17. In schools, females and males are segregated (i.e., kept in separate groups), and this segregation negatively affects classroom communication.

T F 18. Female managers (bosses) are seen as better communicators than male managers by their male and female subordinates (employees).

T F 19. In classroom communications, teachers are more likely to give verbal praise to female students than to male students.

T F 20. In general, men smile more often than women.

Compare your answers to those in the Answers section at the end of the workbook.

Conclusions

1. How do the statements in this survey compare with your own experience of female and male communication patterns?

2. If it is true that women and men in the United States communicate differently, in what ways do you think it might affect their relationships (work, school, friendship, romance)?

3. In which cultures might the answer to a question be different from what you believe to be true for the United States?

Item No.	Culture	Explanation

SOURCE: Reprinted with the permission of Drs. Myra and David Sadker, who use this quiz and other materials in their workshops on sex bias and sexual harassment, which they conduct at schools, colleges, and private corporations. For further information, write Drs. David and Myra Sadker, American University, Washington, DC 20016.

Purpose

To study how women have been shown in advertising

Instructions

Visit a library and find examples of both old and new magazine advertisements that show pictures of women. Also find examples from U.S. magazines and international magazines. In these magazines, look for some ads that are directed toward women and some that are directed toward men. Describe and compare the ads you find.

Conclusions

1. How are the images presented in the advertisements different?

2. In what ways did the older advertisements contribute to stereotyping?

3. In what ways do the new advertisements reflect the culture of origin?

MORE ▷

4. When you compared the ads for men and the ads for women were there any "hidden messages" that suggested how women should behave or be perceived? If so, what were they?

5. Compare the international magazines with the U.S. magazines. Are there any differences in the ways that women are shown? How are women shown in the magazines with a male audience versus how women are shown in the magazines with a female audience?

CHAPTER 13

Contact Between Cultures

When cultures have contact with each other they often learn new ideas and practices from each other. There are two models of how ideas travel from one culture to another: the diffusion model and the convergence model.

Diffusion happens when a culture learns or adopts a new idea or practice. There are two important roles that help a new idea or practice to diffuse into a culture. The first role is opinion leadership. Opinion leadership is held by individuals who can influence other people. These people help change people's behavior and attitudes about the innovation (new idea). The other role is change agent. Change agents have influence over innovation decisions; that is, they help decide whether or not to use a new idea. When a new idea or practice is adopted, some people begin to use it very quickly, whereas others are slow to change. People who use the new idea can be divided into groups depending on how quickly they decided to use the idea. They are innovators, early adopters, early majority, late majority, and laggards. Innovators are often young, well-educated, risk takers, open-minded, and already familiar with the change.

The diffusion process can be seen in the development of quality circles in Japan. The idea of quality circles (a technique for quality control in manufacturing) was developed by a man from the United States. Japanese manufacturing companies borrowed the ideas and successfully adapted the process to Japanese culture. U.S. businesses saw how successful Japan was in using quality circles and decided to use quality circles, too. However, because U.S. businesses did not try to change the practice to fit the U.S. culture, quality circles did not succeed very well (even though quality circles were originally a U.S. idea). It is important, therefore, for the change message (innovation) to be adapted to the new culture.

The convergence model describes a process of sharing information. Over time, individuals from the different cultures come to a greater level of agreement with each other. An example of this is how the idea of democracy was adapted to traditional customs in Bolivia and Botswana.

Although an important part of diffusion is adapting an idea to a new culture, there are times when this is not desirable. For example, in marketing cultural icons (symbols of a culture like "Mickey Mouse" or "Coke") to other cultures it is not desirable to change the idea. What is actually being sold is a "piece" of culture.

When contact occurs between cultures, change can occur in any part of the cultures. This is why many countries do not want too much contact with other cultures. They fear cultural hegemony or the influence that other cultures may have on their own culture. To avoid hegemony, many cultures do things like limiting the kinds and amounts of products from other countries. For example, India did not allow Coke to be sold in its country from 1977 to 1993.

◙ **EXERCISE 13.1: MARKETING CULTURAL ICONS**

Purposes

1. To recognize icons of the United States and other countries
2. To develop an understanding of the diffusion process

Instructions

1. Make a list of recent United States icons that were not mentioned in Chapter 14. Also make a list of icons from other countries that are sold in the United States. If you were born and grew up in another country, you may make a list of icons from your country that are sold in the United States and a list of icons from the United States that are sold in your country.

2. Consider now the characteristics of innovators and how new ideas are adopted by cultures. For every icon that you have listed, try to list the characteristics of the people (or part of the culture) who have adopted it.

U.S. Icons	Characteristics of Adopters
Example: cowboy boots	In Japan: urban college students; young, fashion-minded, educated, previous exposure through media and possibly travel

Icons From Other Countries	Characteristics of Adopters
Example: French perfume	In the United States: upper-middle and upper class women; educated; middle-aged or older; "sophistocated"

EXERCIJE 13.2: ONE CULTURE BECOMEJ TWO

Purposes

1. To examine ways that cultures can develop differently
2. To consider how intercultural communication barriers can occur as cultures develop differently

Instructions

1. Suppose that the state, territory, or province where you live decides to separate from the rest of the country. Consider the ways that it might develop an identity that would be uniquely different from the cultural identity of the rest of the country.

2. Now imagine that your state, territory, or province and the rest of the country reunify 50 years from now. What intercultural communication barriers do you think would have developed?

▣ **EXERCISE 13.3: EXPLAINING THE UNKNOWN**

Purpose

To understand how people interpret the unknown through the established paradigms of their culture

Instructions

1. Read the following description of a well-known event in United States history. Consider what you know of the people and events (and cultural paradigms) from that time and think of why Americans reacted as they did.

2. Read the prompt in Part 2 and answer the questions that follow it.

Part 1

On October 30, 1938, the CBS Mercury Theater on the Air broadcast a radio drama that described a Martian invasion of Earth. This drama was written by Orson Welles and was based on the book, *The War of the Worlds*, written by H. G. Wells. The radio drama was performed in a very realistic manner; it included things like real-sounding news reports, sound effects, the "fake" destruction of the CBS broadcasting station, and descriptions of the destruction of New York City and the people who lived there. This radio broadcast was believed to be true by many people, and it reportedly caused a lot of people to panic. In the drama, the Martians first landed near a city in New Jersey called Grover's Mill. This was an actual city, and it is reported that there were many traffic jams near the "landing site." At this time, in other parts of the world, Hitler was invading Czechoslovakia.

What do you think caused people to react to the story in this way?

Part 2

Suppose now that intelligent life is discovered on one of Jupiter's moons.

1. Imagine the forms that this life might take and describe them. Have these beings formed societies? If so, what patterns do you think they have developed?

2. Discuss your own reactions to the notion that intelligent life might exist elsewhere in the universe.

◻ **EXERCISE 13.4: JAPANESE AND STEREOTYPES**

Purposes

1. To recognize stereotypes of the Japanese
2. To discover Japanese stereotypes of the United States
3. To recognize how these stereotypes affect intercultural communication

Instructions

1. Whether or not you are a member of the group, identify common stereotypes about the Japanese and also stereotypes that the Japanese may have about the United States.
2. Give the sources of those stereotypes.
3. Explain how those stereotypes affect intercultural communication.

Stereotypes About the Japanese	Source	Effect
Example: Protectionist—Won't allow U.S. products to be sold in country	Media	Resentment

Stereotypes About the United States	Source	Effect
Example: U.S. workforce not as productive because of diversity	Media	Superiority

Conclusions

1. What have been the major sources of the stereotypes?

2. How has the stereotype affected intercultural communication?

▣ EXERCISE 13.5: EXPERIENCING INTERCULTURAL COMMUNICATION AS A JAPANESE

Purpose

To experience the communication barriers the Japanese experience in the United States

Instructions

The following statements describe the experience of the Japanese in the United States.

1. What aspects of the Japanese culture do these statements reflect?
2. Describe their effects on intercultural communication.

1. U.S. English speakers seem loud, constantly talking, and too aggressive.
2. U.S. English seems very repetitive. This can sound repetitive.
3. It is difficult to begin conversation because of language problems and feeling self-conscious about making mistakes.
4. In conversations, people speak very fast and do not pause very often. It is difficult—if not impossible—to enter into a conversation.
5. U.S. English speakers rush in to fill pauses or silences in a conversation.
6. It is difficult to disagree with someone verbally.
7. It is difficult to make unilateral decisions (i.e., answers to such questions as "What do you want to do?").
8. It is difficult to read body cues. For example, women cross their legs in the United States. Until recently, this would be very shocking in Japan.
9. Direct eye contact seems accusatory (like someone is trying to blame another person) or aggressive.
10. It is difficult to interpret voice tone. U.S. English speakers use raised voices to indicate enthusiasm or excitement. In Japan, a raised voice means anger.
11. The physical size of U.S. English speakers makes Japanese speakers feel small and weak in comparison.
12. U.S. thinking seems to divide everything into clear, separate categories with no overlap or ambiguities.
13. U.S. English speakers use informal language to older people. This makes Japanese speakers feel uncomfortable.
14. Manners are different. Japanese women often misinterpret U.S. men's manners as kindness and personal interest (romantic interest).
15. Public kissing and touching is very embarrassing.
16. Interacting with minorities in the United States is even more difficult because of differences in accents, vocabulary, voice pitch, and so on.

Aspects of Culture Represented	*Effect on Communication*
Example: Item 5: Silence is appreciated in a high-context culture.	U.S. culture relies more on words.

SOURCE: Statements written by Yosei Sugawara. Used with permission.

CHAPTER 14

Immigration and Acculturation

These days, international travel is becoming more and more common. Some people may stay in a country for a short time; others may stay longer or even permanently. If a person lives in a new culture for some time (typically a few months or more), that individual usually experiences culture shock. Culture shock is used to describe feelings of anxiety and disorientation that come from living in a new culture. Over time, people learn how to live in and adapt to the norms and values of the new culture. This process is called acculturation. There are several things that affect how well a person may acculturate. When a person's home culture is similar to the new culture, it is easier to adjust to the new culture. Generally, younger and better educated people adjust more quickly to a new culture. Also, a person's personality can affect acculturation. Outgoing, curious, and talkative people are often very successful at acculturating. And people who have had contact with the culture before, such as through travel, on television, or in movies, also may acculturate better.

The United States is literally a country of immigrants because for more than 100 years immigration has been encouraged. This policy came from the Pennsylvania Colony's tradition of allowing open immigration. Most people came voluntarily, mostly looking for economic opportunity. However, the largest group of people who came before 1800 did not immigrate by choice. It is estimated that 12 million people were taken to the Americas as slaves. Only about 10 million survived the conditions on the ships.

The years between 1880 and 1919 represent a major period of immigration to the U.S. This period of time has been called the "Melting Pot" era because so many people came to the United States and became citizens. The word that describes this "melting pot" concept is assimilation. When people assimilate into a new culture, they leave their old culture behind. They identify with the new culture, learn the culture's language, and try to participate as a member of the new culture as much as possible.

After every large wave of immigration to the United States, the group of new immigrants experienced discrimination. In the past there was strong pressure to assimilate, and this discrimination may have added to it. However, most of the pressure to assimilate must have come from travel and communication difficulties. It was very difficult to travel between continents, and the mail system was very slow. More recent immigrants to the United States do not feel as much pressure to assimilate. Modern transportation and media allow people to continue to have contact with their old culture. For example, they can visit their home countries, watch television programs in their native languages, and talk on the telephone with friends and family back home.

EXERCISE 14.1: IMMIGRATION INTO THE UNITED STATES ◙

Purposes

1. To appreciate the experience of immigrants into the United States
2. To recognize the effects of culture shock

Instructions

If you are an immigrant (or sojourner) to the United States, answer the following questions for yourself. If not, answer them for any member of your family who immigrated to the United States.

NAME OF PERSON ANSWERING QUESTIONS: _____

COUNTRY OF ORIGIN: _____

1. When did the immigration begin? What were the social, political, and economic conditions of that country at that time?

2. What was the person's acculturation potential? Consider the factors that contribute to a person's successfully acculturating to a new culture (i.e., age, education, previous exposure to language and culture, etc.) and comment on them.

MORE ➡

3. What were the social, political, and economic conditions in the United States at the time of immigration?

4. What symptoms of culture shock did this person experience?

5. What were the major intercultural communication barriers that this person experienced?

CHAPTER 15

Forces Against Assimilation

You may remember that the United States used to be called a "melting pot." This was because people who immigrated to the United States left their old languages and cultures behind and assimilated into the dominant culture. However, assimilation is not the only thing that may happen when people immigrate to a new country. Remember that cultures may exist within cultures. People may become marginalized, experience separation, or integrate. Marginalized people lose their identity and connection with their old culture but do not have meaningful interaction with the new culture. Immigrants may also live separately from the dominant culture and maintain their own cultural identity. This may be voluntary or involuntary. Immigrants who integrate into the dominant society learn the language and values of the dominant culture but also maintain their old language and culture. In this way, they can interact well with both cultures.

An example of marginalized people can be seen in the experience of the Iu Mien and the Hmong refugees. Because of war, they were isolated from their home culture. Since they did not speak English, they were also isolated from the U.S. culture.

The Amish people are an example of how a culture can live in separation from the dominant society. The Amish live in farming communities and maintain cultural values that are quite different from dominant American cultural values. One of the biggest differences is that the Amish limit their use of technology and accept change slowly.

Historically, Asian immigrants to the United States experienced separation. A well-known example of this kind of treatment was the internment of Japanese-Americans during World War II. Recently, however, Asian-Americans have experienced more integration. Two areas that have helped Asian-Americans have stronger cultural identities are specialized media and segmented marketing. Specialized media include Asian-American magazines, newspapers, radio, and television. Segmented marketing is done by businesses that want to sell their products to Asian-Americans. These businesses use their knowledge of Asian cultures and languages to help them advertise and do business in Asian-American communities.

▣ EXERCISE 15.1: ORAL HISTORY INTERVIEWS

Purpose

To learn more about the history of cultures and subgroups from their members

Instructions

Arrange to interview a person who is somewhat older than you and who is from a culture or group that you are not a member of.

NAME OF PERSON: _____

CULTURE OR GROUP: _____

The following question areas are suggested:

1. How long ago can the person remember?

2. What does the person remember of the experiences of being an immigrant or subgroup member in that time?

3. What does the person recall of the communication with members of the dominant culture?

4. What types of changes does the person think have been most significant?

5. Other comments:

Conclusions

From this interview, what can you conclude about earlier days of immigration or subgroup identification?

CHAPTER 16

Forces to Conform to One Cultural Identity

ategories are useful for helping people define and understand things. Often, people place themselves in a category, and from that category they gain identity. But sometimes people are placed in categories or are forced to choose one they would not choose for themselves. This has been the experience of many Hispanic people in the United States. When Hispanics apply for a job or fill out official forms like the U.S. Census form (the Census counts and categorizes all the people living in the United States), they often must indicate their ethnic identity. The choices provided are very limited, and so Hispanic people often must report an ethnic identity that they really do not identify with.

Some people in the United States often do not realize that the Hispanic culture includes people from many different countries and ethnic backgrounds. For example, many immigrants are actually American Indians (ethnic background) but come from Mexico (country of origin). Also, people who identify with being Hispanic may or may not speak Spanish. A mistake often made is assuming that people can speak Spanish just because they have Spanish-sounding last names.

Recently, a lot of attention has been given to the number of Hispanic immigrants coming into the United States and the effect that this influx may have on the country. However, Hispanic people and culture are not new to the United States, for Hispanic people lived in the southwestern region of North America even before it was a part of the United States. Hispanic culture is already a large part of the culture of this region of the United States.

In the past in the United States, there was a lot of pressure for people to assimilate into the dominant culture. Today, however, the pressure is not as strong. Two areas that help Hispanic people maintain a cultural identity in the United States are specialized media and segmented marketing. Specialized media include Hispanic magazines, newspapers, radio, and television. These media generally use the Spanish language and focus on things that are important to the Hispanic community. Advertising also helps continue and strengthen the culture.

Purposes

1. To recognize stereotypes of Hispanic people
2. To recognize how these stereotypes affect intercultural communication

Instructions

1. Whether or not you are a member of the group, identify stereotypes about Hispanic people.
2. Give the sources of those stereotypes.
3. Explain how these stereotypes affect intercultural communication.

Stereotypes About Hispanic People	*Source*	*Effect*
Example: Hispanic women are submissive.	Old movies	Excludes women from positions of power

Conclusions

1. What have been the major sources of the stereotypes?

2. How have the stereotypes affected intercultural communication?

▣ **EXERCISE 16.2: USING NEW CULTURAL KNOWLEDGE**

Purpose

To use knowledge of the Hispanic subculture to examine intercultural communication situations

Instructions

Read and analyze the incident described below. Consider such things as what cultural values are being reflected and how the incident could have been avoided or handled differently.

> Alicia's teacher wrote some English words on the blackboard. Alicia did not understand what many of the words meant. She asked her teacher, but the teacher told her to ask her at the end of the school day. At that time, however, there were many other children who were waiting for the teacher to help them. Alicia went home and did not wait to ask the teacher about the words she had not understood.

SOURCE: Adapted from R. D. Albert, "Mexican-American Children in Educational Settings: Research on Children's and Teachers' Perceptions and Interpretations of Behavior," quoted in Rosita Daskal Albert, "The Intercultural Sensitizer or Culture Assimilator: A Cognitive Approach," in Dan Landis and Richard W. Brislin (Eds.), *Handbook of Intercultural Training, Volume II* (New York: Pergamon, 1983), p. 194.

EXERCISE 16.3: EXPERIENCING BILINGUALISM   ▣

Purpose

To experience shifting from one language to another

Instructions

1. If you are not bilingual, read the following selection aloud.
2. Answer the questions that follow.

Line 1: Perhaps you will never answer my letters.
Line 2: *Ya nada espero ni pido nada.*
Line 3: Wouldn't it be absurd to ask the mailman
Line 4: *si me trae un sobre que brilla*
Line 5: like a tiny star?

SOURCE: "Poesia Última, translated by Leslie Keffer, in Nora Jacquez Wieser (Ed.), *Open to the Sun: A Bilingual Anthology of Latin-American Women Poets* (Van Nuys, CA: Perivale Press, 1979), pp. 74-75. Reprinted with permission.

English translation:

Line 2: At this age I don't hope or ask for anything.
Line 4: if he's bringing a letter that shines

Conclusions

1. Describe your ability to communicate in the language you did not know.

2. Describe how you might feel about yourself as a communicator if you had to communicate in the language you did not know.

▣ EXERCISE 16.4: MEXICAN PROVERBS

Purpose

To discover Mexican values through proverbs

Instructions

Proverbs can be defined as short, pithy epigrammatic statements that set forth a general well-known truth. They then communicate the opinions, feelings, manners, or customs of a community of people.

1. Determine the message of each of the proverbs below.
2. What does the proverb tell you about the people?
3. Think of a contrasting proverb from another culture.

Ganar un pleito es adquirir un pollo y perder una vaca. [To win a dispute is to gain a chicken and lose a cow.]

La amistad sincera es un alma repartida en dos cuerpos. [True friendship is one soul shared by two bodies.]

De médico, poeta, músico y loco todos tenemos un poco. [Of doctor and poet, musician and madman, we each have a trace.]

El sol es la cobija del pobre. [The sun is the blanket of the poor.]

Un hombre sin alegría no es bueno o no está bueno. [A man without happiness is either not good or not well.]

SOURCE: *The Folk Wisdom of Mexico* (San Francisco: Chronicle Books, 1994).

CHAPTER 17

Reclaiming a Culture

What's in a name? Certainly, we have seen that words have the power to influence our perceptions of reality. Names and labels are important because they help define our identities. African-Americans are one group whose label has changed over time. In the past, people used the words Negroes and Blacks. Now many people use the word African-American. These labels reflect the history and experience of African-Americans in the United States. African-Americans experienced slavery, segregation (separation from the dominant culture), integration (an end of separation and forced interaction with the dominant culture), and being a culture within a culture.

African worldview includes the beliefs that the spiritual world and the physical world are one and that religion is a central part of life. African worldview also includes beliefs that nature and the universe exist in harmony, that society should follow natural patterns, and that time is cyclical. Afrocentrism is the belief that the history, culture, and behavior of Blacks around the world is an extension of African history and culture. An Afrocentrist might see a communication style (which emphasizes verbal ability) and strong involvement in churches and communities as coming from African culture. African-American culture in the United States is constructed. It has grown from the efforts of African-Americans to recover the culture that was lost during slavery. Things that support African-American cultural identity are media and marketing, special schools, and holidays like Kwanzaa.

Purpose

To consider the importance of labeling

Instructions

Below are some labels that African-Americans have used or had applied to them. Put the labels in historical order from oldest to the most recent.

____ African-American
____ Afro-American
____ Black
____ Black American
____ Colored
____ Negro
____ People of color

Conclusions

1. What is the origin of each label?

2. What are the positive and negative qualities associated with each label?

3. What is the focus of each label?

◎ **EXERCISE 17.2: AFRICAN-AMERICAN PROVERBS**

Purpose

To discover early African-American values through proverbs

Instructions

Proverbs can be defined as short, pithy epigrammatic statements that set forth a general well-known truth. They then communicate the opinions, feelings, manners, or customs of a community of people.

1. Determine the message of each of the proverbs below.
2. What does the proverb tell you about the people?
3. Think of a contrasting proverb from another culture.

You got eyes to see and wisdom not to see.

Muddy roads call the mile post a liar.

Every bell ain't a dinner bell.

A mule can tote so much goodness in his face that he don't have none left for his hind legs.

The graveyard is the cheapest boarding house.

SOURCE: Adapted from Sandra Tijitendero, "Proverbs," in David S. Hoopes and Paul Ventura (Eds.), *Intercultural Sourcebook: Cross-Cultural Training Methodologies* (Chicago: Intercultural Press, 1979), pp. 168-169.

▣ **EXERCISE 17.3: AFRICAN-AMERICANS IN ADVERTISING**

Purpose

To study how African-Americans have been shown in advertising

Instructions

Visit a library and find examples of old magazine advertisements that show African-Americans. Also look in contemporary magazines directed especially toward African-Americans. Describe and compare the ads you find.

Conclusions

1. How are the images presented in the advertisements different?

2. In what ways did the older advertisements contribute to stereotyping?

3. In what ways do the new advertisements contribute to a co-culture identity?

CHAPTER 18

Identity and Subgroups

R ecall that language affects and is affected by culture. Every language is unique. It reflects how its speakers see reality, and, in turn, it controls how its speakers perceive and talk about reality. You may also remember that cultures and subcultures have their own languages; however, subgroups, too, may have their own special way of communicating. This is called "argot" (pronounced AR-go), which is a special vocabulary. In the past, this kind of special vocabulary had names like "jargon," "cant," and "slang." However, argot is a term that includes these meanings and does not have the negative meanings that some of the other words have. Argot has two functions. First, it helps members of a subgroup create a feeling of identity with the subgroup. Second, it helps members know who is in their group and who is not.

Subgroups often have their own argot. Members of subgroups may communicate with each other through special media like magazines and newspapers. However, the most important element of a subgroup is that it provides its members with a set of values and norms for behavior. Recall that people may be members of many subgroups throughout their lives. Often, they are members of different subgroups at the same time.

The term "corporate culture" refers to how organizations behave like little cultures. One definition of corporate culture is "the way we do things around here." This shows that corporations provide their members with norms that control behavior. Often, organizations have their own argot and have the values of the organization's founder. Walt Disney Productions and Microsoft are two examples of corporations that have a special culture.

In the United States, homosexual people are a unique subgroup based on sexual orientation. Gays (homosexual men) and lesbians (homosexual women) show an awareness of subgroup identity. This identity is becoming stronger partly through the effects of segmented marketing and specialized media. Within the gay community, "coming out" (being openly gay) is seen as a very important part of a gay person's identity. This has positive and negative aspects. On one hand, being openly gay allows a person to receive emotional support from other gay individuals. On the other hand, an openly gay individual may become a victim of discrimination and violence ("gay bashing"). Being afraid of and hating homosexual people is called "homophobia."

Purposes

1. To appreciate how specific and complete subgroup argot can become
2. To discover how argot relates to subgroup activities and interests

Instructions

Match the argot in Column A to the subgroup who uses it in Column B and to its definition in Column C. Compare your answers to those in the Answers section at the end of the workbook.

Column A	Column B	Column C
___ 1. air	a. advertising	a. beach goer with a very pale complexion
___ 2. airtime	b. business/finance	
___ 3. asphalt surfer	c. computers	b. beginning surfer with head in kelp
___ 4. baby catcher	d. crime	
___ 5. barney	e. dentists	c. bloods
___ 6. bogon	f. fashion	d. blue (Crips) or red (Bloods) bandanna to show group affiliation
___ 7. casper	g. film	
___ 8. crabs	h. gangs	e. bullion coin minted by Canada
___ 9. cubed out	i. media	f. clothing manufacturer who copies a well-known designer
___ 10. do-rag	j. medical	
___ 11. drilling, filling, and billing	k. military	g. clueless
	l. real estate	h. Crips
___ 12. fade the heat	m. roller coaster	i. filled to capacity
___ 13. flash and trash	n. ski instructors	j. flattering article about client
___ 14. green alert	o. surfing	k. height on a jump
___ 15. kelphead		l. know-it-all student
___ 16. killer bees		m. know-it-all student
___ 17. knock-off artist		n. money budgeted for perks for top talent
___ 18. Maple Leaf		
___ 19. NIMBY		o. near-zero gravity
___ 20. puff piece		p. "not in my backyard" said by those who oppose certain projects
___ 21. rev-head		
___ 22. slobs		q. obstetrician
___ 23. star baggage		r. one who thinks cars are more important than surfboards
___ 24. trout		
___ 25. wire bender		s. orthodontist
		t. outsiders used to help fight takeover
		u. person who says bogus things
		v. skateboarder
		w. take responsibility
		x. the dental business
		y. warning that someone is getting sick on a ride

MORE →

Conclusions

1. What forms the basis of argot?

2. What does the argot reveal about the subgroup?

SOURCES: *Slang! The Topic-by-Topic Contemporary American Lingoes* (Pocket Books) and *The Surfin'ary: A Dictionary of Surfing Terms and Surfspeak* (Trevor Cralle; Ten Speed Press, 1991).

EXERCIƒE 18.2: LEƒBIANƒ AND GAY MEN AND ƒTEREOTYPEƒ   ▣

Purposes

1. To recognize stereotypes of lesbians and gay men
2. To recognize how those stereotypes affect intercultural communication

Instructions

1. Whether or not you are a member of the group, identify stereotypes of lesbians and gay men.
2. Give the sources of those stereotypes.
3. Explain how those stereotypes affect intercultural communication.

Stereotypes About Lesbians and Gay Men	Source	Effect
Example: All homosexuals are HIV positive.	Friends	Fear of contact

Conclusions

1. What have been the major sources of the stereotypes?

2. How have the stereotypes affected intercultural communication?

▣ **EXERCISE 18.3: SCHOOL OR EMPLOYMENT CULTURE**

Purposes

1. To recognize how one's school or place of employment can be viewed as a culture
2. To describe the special communication behavior of that culture

Instructions

Answer the following questions about your school or place of employment.

NAME OF GROUP BEING DESCRIBED: _____

1. Identify when and where communication usually takes place.

2. Identify any shared argot. If there is more than one argot spoken in this place, identify which groups speak each argot.

3. Identify any shared nonverbals (i.e., dress codes, symbols, etc.).

4. Describe how the communication changes depending on who the receiver is.

5. Identify the typical content of conversations.

6. From the content, identify values and goals shared by the speakers of the argot.

7. Identify the media that are used to communicate those values and goals.

Conclusions

What insights about your school or place of employment became clear when you viewed it as a culture?

CHAPTER 19

Multiculturalism

The United States has been described as a multicultural society. In the past, people acculturated (adjusted) to American society by assimilating into the dominant culture. To do this, they lost their old cultures and learned the language and culture of the United States. This was the idea of the "melting pot," where everybody became American. Today, people acculturate to the dominant culture by integrating. They learn the dominant culture and language of the United States but do not lose their original cultures.

If the United States is a multicultural society, is there then a dominant U.S. culture, or are there just a lot of "little cultures"? The answer is that there is a dominant culture and a definite power structure. The dominant culture represents the values of heterosexual White males. Communication aspects of this culture include the use of Standard English, direct eye contact, limited physical contact, and controlled expression of emotions. Economic and political power is generally held in U.S. society by youthful (at least in appearance), healthy (not physically disabled), heterosexual White males. Other people hold power, but they have the same values as the heterosexual White males. The special advantage that White males have in the power structure has been called "white privilege." Nondominant groups find it difficult to share power in this structure.

All people live in and identify with many different groups at the same time. A postethnic perspective recognizes this fact. Instead of having identities based on things like ethnicity (rigid, inflexible), it encourages people to have identities that they choose for themselves and that are based on their affiliations (changing, flexible). The postethnic perspective is idealistic because people still label each other (i.e., give names like Black or Hispanic) and communicate with each other according to these labels.

The special communication problems for multicultural societies come from culture shock, conflicting values, discrimination, and multiple language use. Culture shock can be very difficult as new immigrants learn to "survive" in the new culture and learn the language. It is often hard to tell how much a person has assimilated into the dominant culture, and so there can be misunderstandings about values. New immigrants and minority group members often face discrimination. There is an obvious problem in communicating for people who do not speak each other's languages. However, there is also a problem of unconscious prejudice against people who do not speak the majority language perfectly.

EXERCISE 19.1: COMMUNICATION AND WHITE CULTURE ▣

Purposes

1. To compare the components of White culture with dominant United States cultural patterns
2. To recognize the intercultural communication challenges within the United States

Instructions

Use Chapters 10 and 19 as a basis to answer the following questions.

1. Compare the components of White culture in Chapter 19 to the dominant United States cultural patterns in Chapter 10.

2. In what ways are the components of White culture reflected in schools and colleges and universities?

3. In what ways are the components of White culture reflected in business organizations?

MORE ▷

4. What communication difficulties can an individual who does not identify with White culture have in schools and colleges and universities?

5. What communication difficulties can an individual who does not identify with White culture have in business organizations?

EXERCISE 19.2: WHITE PRIVILEGE   ▣

Purpose

To understand how being a member of the dominant culture benefits its members in unseen ways

Instructions

In Chapter 19, a partial list of the benefits of being a member of the dominant group in the United States was presented. Make a list of other benefits that were not mentioned in the chapter. If you are not a member of a U.S. group, make a list for the dominant group in your culture.

CULTURE: _____   DOMINANT GROUP:_____

Dominant Group Benefits

Conclusions

Whether or not you are a member of the dominant group, how have your own experiences either validated or invalidated the notion of White privilege (or dominant-group privilege)?

CHAPTER 20

Challenges Facing Intercultural Communication

I t's a small world after all. As companies expand globally, there is more and more interaction between people of different cultures. The problems that one or a few countries face have the potential to affect other countries. Some of the problems that the world now faces and likely will continue to in the future are population, distribution of wealth, and ethnic conflict.

In countries such as Japan and the United States, the population is aging; that is, there is a growing number of people over the age of 60. This will affect the societies and economies of these countries. Other population issues include the fertility rate (how many children people have) and the effects of AIDS. In some countries like Japan and Denmark, the fertility rate is so low that the population is actually declining. Any population growth in these countries will have to come from immigration. Most of the world's population growth is occurring in developing countries. Rwanda, for example, has a fertility rate of 8.5 children per woman. Many of these developing countries face the additional problem of having an AIDS epidemic because they are so poor that they cannot buy drugs to fight the virus. Unequal distribution of wealth continues to be a problem. The richest 20% of the world's population controls 85% of the world's resources. High population growth rates in the poorest countries make the problem of poverty even worse. In other countries, such as some of the former Soviet republics, ethnic conflicts (race wars) have begun and more may happen in the future.

Becoming a competent intercultural communicator involves learning and appreciating the uniqueness of other people and cultures. However, you do not need to feel ashamed of or not apprciate your own culture. Good intercultural communicators uses their knowledge to select message behavior that is appropriate and effective for that context.

Purpose

To relate the course material to your own life history

Instructions

1. Think back to an intercultural experience you have had which in some way has been significant to you.

2. Analyze that experience using the material from the course and text.

My Experience

Conclusions

1. What may have led up to the experience?

2. Reframe the experience by applying some of the concepts of this course to the situation.

3. How did that experience affect you?

Purpose

To plan a course of action to improve one's own intercultural communication skills

Instructions

1. Using the intercultural communication skills identified in Chapter 2, assess your current strengths and weaknesses.
2. Identify those areas you need to improve.
3. Identify specific steps to take to improve in these areas.

Personal Assessment

Development Plan

Answers

Exercise 1.6

1. e	6. c	11. a	16. b
2. e	7. b	12. d	17. a
3. e	8. e	13. e	18. a
4. a	9. e	14. a	19. d
5. b	10. a	15. e	20. b

Exercise 6.1

Part 1

1. g	8. b	15. s	22. cc	29. c
2. bb	9. dd	16. gg	23. x	30. d
3. ff	10. e	17. ii	24. p	31. l
4. f	11. n	18. w	25. i	32. aa
5. q	12. z	19. j	26. y	33. u
6. m	13. r	20. a	27. k	34. hh
7. o	14. v	21. ee	28. t	35. h

Part 2

1. e	4. b	7. j	10. i
2. k	5. f	8. g	11. d
3. a	6. c	9. h	12. l

MORE

Exercise 6.3

Part 1

1. o	6. l	11. n	16. f	21. v
2. g	7. q	12. x	17. b	22. j
3. h	8. k	13. r	18. s	23. w
4. i	9. d	14. m	19. t	24. c
5. p	10. a	15. e	20. u	

Part 2

1. g	6. i	11. b	16. c
2. m	7. p	12. o	17. a
3. e	8. h	13. f	
4. k	9. j	14. d	
5. q	10. l	15. n	

Exercise 7.2

1. b	6. c	11. e	16. m
2. a	7. g	12. d	17. r
3. s	8. h	13. o	18. n
4. f	9. q	14. j	19. p
5. i	10. k	15. l	20. t

Exercise 9.3

English equivalents: These are not perfect equivalents; their shortcomings, though, can serve to highlight cultural differences.

1. The English "Don't make waves" seems to emphasize moderation rather than conformity.
2. "Everything has its place" but it doesn't seem to emphasize modesty as the Japanese proverb does.
3. "The land outlasts the king."
4. "Anybody can make a mistake."
5. Possibly "Familiarity breeds contempt" but it doesn't emphasize manners as the Japanese proverb does.
6. "The mouth is the gate of evil" and "Loose lips sink ships."
7. "Don't wash dirty linen in public."
8. The English "Children are a burden to their parents" doesn't fully capture the Buddhist-based meaning.

Exercise 12.1

1. True	6. False	11. True	16. False
2. True	7. False	12. True	17. True
3. False	8. False	13. True	18. True
4. True	9. False	14. True	19. False
5. True	10. True	15. True	20. False

AUTHORS' NOTE: Recent research has called into question the answers given for Items 2 and 15.

Exercise 18.1

1. n, k	6. c, u	11. e, x	16. b, t	21. o, r
2. m, o	7. o, a	12. d, w	17. f, f	22. h, c
3. o, v	8. h, h	13. i, m	18. b, e	23. g, n
4. j, q	9. k, i	14. m, y	19. l, p	24. n, l
5. o, g	10. h, d	15. o, b	20. a, j	25. e, s